CW00496413

Rockley Wilson
Remarkable Cricketer, Singular Man

Martin Howe

First published in Great Britain by
Association of Cricket Statisticians and Historians
Cardiff CF11 9XR
© ACS, 2008

British Library Cataloguing-in-Publication Data.
A catalogue record for this book is available from the British Library.

ISBN: 978 1 905138 57 9
Typeset by Limlow Books

Contents

Rockley Wilson, 'fully kitted',
taken by Abram Waddington at Scarborough in 1922.
Yorkshire won the Championship this year, with Rockley taking over
the captaincy from Geoffrey Wilson in early August.

Chapter One
The Wilson Family

One thousand feet above sea level in the southern Pennines, and nine miles north-west of Sheffield, lies the small and ancient village of Bolsterstone. In 1867 William Reginald Wilson was appointed vicar at Bolsterstone and during the ensuing 29 years his wife presented him with eight children, three daughters and five sons. Nothing remarkable about that: large families were commonplace in Victorian England. But what is remarkable is that all five sons were to make their mark in one capacity or another in the world of cricket.

Two of the boys, Clement Eustace Macro, usually known as Clem, and the youngest, Evelyn Rockley, born on 25 March, 1879 and always known as Rockley, were to distinguish themselves in the first-class game. Both played for Cambridge University and Yorkshire and also for England, albeit only twice in the case of Clement and but a single time in that of Rockley. These are not remarkable achievements in themselves. What makes Rockley's first-class cricket career remarkable is that it began in 1899 at the height of cricket's Golden Age, went into abeyance when he became a schoolteacher at Winchester College in 1903 until, effectively, after the First World War, and ended 24 years later in 1923 when Rockley was 44 years old. Moreover, Rockley was one of the game's personalities "in a day", as *The Times* put it in an obituary, "when the word had not been debased." With a ready wit and an impish sense of humour, there are more anecdotes involving Rockley Wilson than perhaps any other cricketer. It is this as much as his performances on the field of play that makes Rockley Wilson so interesting – and challenging – a subject for a biography.

Family background

From their beginnings as yeomen in the ancient Manor of Bolsterstone, the Wilson family had acquired sizeable estates in the area. By the eighteenth century the Wilsons were a family "of superior station" as a local history put it.[1] The family seat was Broomhead Hall, situated some two miles from the village of Bolsterstone on the edge of Broomhead Moor. A notable owner of Broomhead Hall and its estates in the eighteenth century was John Wilson, who was known as The Antiquarian in recognition of his historical interests and scholarship. A younger son of The Antiquarian, William Wilson, established a successful wine business in Sheffield. William's own younger son, James, was born in 1789 and became a solicitor in Sheffield and took a prominent part in civic affairs and in the Cutlers' Company. James and his wife Elizabeth had three sons. The third of these, William Reginald born in 1838, was to be Rockley Wilson's father.

Before we continue the story of Rockley Wilson's immediate family, it will be helpful to trace something of the history of the main branch of the Wilson family, for in due course the owners of Broomhead Hall were to become neighbours as well as relatives of William Reginald Wilson and his own family. We need to revert to James Wilson, Rockley Wilson's paternal grandfather. In 1814 he entered into partnership with another successful Sheffield lawyer John Rimington.

In 1802, John Rimington had purchased the manor, freehold and tithe-free estate of Bolsterstone from Lord Melbourne, Queen Victoria's Prime Minister and the latest of a succession of nobles and notables who had been Lord of the Manor of Bolsterstone down the centuries.[2] The manor lands were then broken up, although the rights and duties that went with the position of Lord of the Manor, including the patron of the local church, and for a time at least the title, continued to be enjoyed by John Rimington and his successors.

John Rimington was married to Mary Wilson who was the sister of Henry Wilson, a merchant living in London and a nephew of the Antiquarian's eldest son, John, the owner of Broomhead Hall. When this John Wilson died without children his wife sold the Broomhead estate in 1810 to Henry Wilson. Henry Wilson never married and when he died in 1819 he bequeathed the estate to

---

1   R.A.Leader, *Sheffield in the Eighteenth Century*, Sheffield Independent Press, 1901, p.6.
2   In the fourteenth century the Lord of the Manor had been Sir Robert de Rockley of Rockley near Barnsley: there is a corbel representing Sir Robert in the church at Bolsterstone. This historical connection more than likely explains his parents' choice of Rockley as one of the Christian names of their youngest son.

James Rimington, a barrister, the only son of Henry's sister Mary and her husband, John Rimington. John died in 1820 and Mary in 1838. One of James Rimington's projects was to complete the rebuilding of the old Hall which dated from 1640. The work, including the landscaping of the adjoining park, was completed in 1831. The new Hall, the third to occupy the site, was large and stately as befitted the home of a successful and prosperous Victorian gentleman.

James Rimington died in 1839. His successor, another James, adopted the surname Rimington-Wilson in accordance with the bequest of Henry Wilson. It is in relation to this James Rimington-Wilson that we find the first mention of cricket in the family history. In 1849, James Rimington-Wilson took into his employment at Broomhead Hall, Edwin (Ned) Stephenson, then a seventeen year old lad but destined to become a Yorkshire cricketer of some renown, playing in 82 first-class matches, including 42 for the county between 1861 and 1873. He was one of the party of English cricketers that made the first tour of Australia in 1861/62.

We know little of Stephenson's role at Broomhead Hall. Since James Rimington-Wilson was then unmarried, Stephenson would not have been employed to coach any sons. Stephenson, who stayed in his post for three years, remarked that he was grateful to his employer "for his first introduction to the cricket field."[3] This shows that by the middle of the nineteenth century there was an active interest in cricket even in small rural communities such as Bolsterstone. We know that in the 1880s there was a Broomhead Cricket Club, presumably drawing on members of the Broomhead Hall household (which at this time numbered ninety people) as well as villagers, and also a Bolsterstone Cricket Club, based in the village and playing its matches at Hagg Field, now home to the Bolsterstone Rugby Club. There was also a cricket club and field in Wigtwizzle, a small village between Bolsterstone and Broomhead Hall. These clubs may well have been founded earlier in the century for, as the game spread from its rural beginnings in the south east to the Midlands and the North, Sheffield became a major centre of cricket and by the 1820s a host of cricket clubs had been established in the town and surrounding villages. As well as playing for the Broomhead club, Ned Stephenson was probably

---

3   Arthur Haygarth, *Cricket Scores and Biographies*, Vol V, 1855 to 1876, Longmans and Co., 1876, p.357.

employed as groundsman and net bowler. There is no record of there being a cricket field on the Broomhead estate.

After the death of James Rimington-Wilson in 1877, the estate passed to his son Reginald Henry Rimington-Wilson, a military man whose main outdoor interests were the usual pursuits of a Victorian country gentleman - hunting, fishing and particularly grouse-shooting. The Squire of Bolsterstone, as he was known, was a popular figure around the village. Reginald Henry was the incumbent of Broomhead Hall at the time that Rockley Wilson was growing up and the family would have been regular visitors to the Hall. Reginald Henry never married and died in 1927, Rockley Wilson being among the family mourners at his funeral. He was succeeded by his nephew, Henry Edmund Rimington-Wilson, another military man. Henry Edmund preferred to live in London however, and visited Broomhead Hall only intermittently. During the Second World War the Hall was used by the military. After the war it fell into disrepair and was eventually demolished in 1980. Only a few foundation stones remain as reminders of a once handsome property. Ben Rimington-Wilson, a descendant of the last inhabitant of Broomhead Hall, lives in a cottage nearby.

Rockley's family

We must now follow this rather complicated family background with an account of Rockley Wilson's own family. William Reginald Wilson, Rockley's father, was educated at Sheffield Collegiate School, a private school established in 1835, and then at Harrow and Trinity College, Cambridge. He was chosen for his house cricket team at Harrow and he may well have played some cricket at Cambridge. After graduation, he probably continued to play for the Collegiate School cricket club, which fielded sides consisting of pupils, masters and old boys. He was a keen follower of the game, frequently walking the few miles from the family home, Brincliffe Towers, to the Bramall Lane ground, which opened in 1855, to watch matches between local clubs.

Like many younger sons of well-to-do families in Victorian England, William Reginald Wilson entered the church after completing his University studies. In 1865 he married Martha Thorp, whose father had played once for Yorkshire, at Barnsley in 1862. After a period as curate, in 1867, as already noted, William became vicar of Bolsterstone, where his relation James

Rimington-Wilson was the Lord of the Manor and patron of the church, the family connection presumably having much to do with the appointment. In that sense the Reverend Wilson was a "society" clergyman. But during his long Ministry he served his congregation and the wider community well and was very popular with the villagers. The value of his work was recognised when in 1899 William was made an honorary canon of York Minster. He remained at Bolsterstone until his death in 1914.

Victorian family holiday.
A photograph taken at Llandudno, probably in 1889.
Back row (l to r): Charles Macro Wilson (Rockley's uncle), Cyril Reynold Wilson (brother). Middle row: Havis (sister), Elizabeth Mary Wilson (aunt), Rev William Reginald Wilson (father), Martha Wilson (née Thorp, mother). Front row: Phyllis (sister), Rockley, Reginald Thorp Wilson (brother).
Brothers Rowland and Clem are missing.

There had been a chapel at Bolsterstone in the parish of Ecclesfield since the fifteenth century, originally the private chapel of the de Rockley family. In due course the chapel came to be used for village worship. Subsequently more substantial village churches were erected. Shortly after his appointment as vicar, William Reginald Wilson set about replacing the then existing church, known as Bland's Church and described in a local brochure as "remarkable for its bare, ugly appearance" and "barn-like, cold and draughty" with a new building. Construction began in 1872 and the new church of St Mary's was completed, at a total cost of £7,200, in 1879, the year of Rockley's birth. Across the road from the church was the vicarage, a substantial two-gabled, three-storied building, set in extensive grounds with views across the moors to Broomhead Hall about two miles away. The vicarage provided ample accommodation and play area for the growing Wilson family. The building is now a private residence but is little changed structurally from the time of the Wilsons' occupancy.

The cricketing Wilsons

William Reginald instilled in all five of his sons an abiding interest in cricket. Often one or more of the boys would accompany their father to watch matches at Bramall Lane or other local grounds. Rockley recalled watching some of the greats of cricket's early years and being struck by the colourful attire of some of the players: "As a boy, I saw Mr A.N.Hornby play there in a starched pink shirt. Lord Harris used to wear an evening shirt and bow tie. P.J.de Paravicini, wearing a sweater with horizontal stripes of red, black and gold [the colours of I Zingari] was cheered to the echo every time he moved, and Middlesex players wore pink shirts. Certainly no players were more smartly turned out than Lord Hawke and Sir Stanley Jackson who used hunting paste to clean their pads." Rockley also recalled his delight at being served with pudding in the public luncheon room at Bramall Lane by Louis Hall, the Yorkshire opener[4] – hardly a chore that would be undertaken by a professional cricketer today. Aside from watching cricket, Clem and Rockley, sometimes joined by an older brother, spent many hours playing cricket on the vicarage lawn. We can assume that it was here that Rockley began to develop the essentials of his cricketing skills, playing straight when batting,

---

4 M.A.Marston, *A Century of Cricket at Bramall Lane, 1855-1955*, Greenup and Wilson (published for Sheffield United Cricket Club), 1955, p.15.

and bowling accurately. He always maintained that a boy had to learn the rudiments of the game before he was ten years old if he was to have any chance of being successful.

Of those brothers, it is appropriate here to say something first about Clem who was born in 1875. He was an outstanding cricketer as a schoolboy at Uppingham School, where he was coached by H.H.Stephenson. He was in the First XI in 1891 at the tender age of fifteen. In 1893 he scored 722 runs for the school at an average of 90.25, with three successive hundreds, including an unbeaten 183 against Repton, when he carried his bat through the innings. He was captain in 1894. Going up to Trinity College, Cambridge in 1895, he won his Blue as a freshman. He scored 115 against Oxford in 1898 the year when he was Cambridge's captain. For many years he held the record for the most runs scored in the annual Varsity match. Clem was also a more than useful right-arm medium-paced bowler. He was also able to bowl left-handed, a facility he had acquired in the vicarage garden at Bolsterstone, and he once bowled both right and left-handed in the same first-class match, for Cambridge against Surrey at The Oval in 1895. After his first season at Cambridge, Clem Wilson was one of the party that Frank Mitchell took to America in 1895. Between 1896 and 1899, he played nine times for Yorkshire and he toured South Africa in 1898/99 with Lord Hawke's team, appearing in two Test Matches there, though he was always amused that the matches were retrospectively given Test match status. In the Second Test, at Cape Town, he batted at No 4 in England's first innings and ran out of partners when only 10 not out. He soon gave up first-class cricket to take up holy orders and was ordained in 1901. Clem did not abandon cricket entirely however. He played occasionally in club cricket and for clergy teams. In the 1920s, on leading a rather venerable Yorkshire Clergy team on to the field at Old Trafford in a match against the Lancashire Clergy, he remarked: "I think we ought to sing 'O God our help in ages past.'" Clearly Clem had some of the wit for which his brother Rockley was better known.

We shall have much to say about Rockley's remarkable cricket career shortly. Suffice here to set the scene and say something about his abilities at the game. Rockley Wilson was of medium height and build with a rather boyish countenance. This makes him easily recognisable in team photographs, often with his cap pulled rather low over his eyes and the collar of his jacket turned up. A more formal portrait photograph of him in his thirties shows a confident looking, fresh-faced young man, clean-shaven, hair neatly brushed and parted, looking steadily into the camera with just the suggestion of a smile about his lips.

As to his cricket, he was a sound, orthodox batsman with a good defensive technique. His stance, with a pronounced bend of the right knee at the crease, was rather inelegant but he played with an impeccably straight bat. When it came to attacking strokes, he was essentially a leg-side player. In a serious match he was reluctant to take any risk at the crease but in club cricket he was more relaxed and could indulge

*Rockley Wilson
in his thirties.*

in some dashing strokeplay. In his early years he was an early-order batsman, often opening the innings, but later in his first-class career he never aspired to be more than a tail-end batsman. His limited range of strokes in these later years is illustrated by one story about him. Playing against Surrey at The Oval, Rockley had deflected a ball to fine leg for a single and a wild return resulted in four overthrows. Emmott Robinson remarked that this was Wilson's first four in front of the wicket since the war!

It was as a bowler that Rockley Wilson made his cricketing name. He was a right-arm slow bowler who turned the ball from leg with finger spin. His variations were the ball that went straight on and occasionally, when delivered from wide of the crease, one that turned from the off. He had a low arm action but objected strongly if his action was described as round-arm – though *Wisden* so described it in 1914. He relied less on spin for his wickets than on his control of length, pace and flight. Especially on hard wickets, Rockley had the technique to make his slower, more flighted deliveries bounce rather higher, and with more pace, than the batsman expected. Arthur Dolphin, the Yorkshire wicketkeeper, referred to these as "Mr Wilson's tennis balls." Bowlers of Rockley Wilson's particular type are not to be seen in today's cricket, certainly at first-class level. His accuracy was legendary. His standard, he once said, was to be able, when loosened up, to pitch a ball five times out of six on an old Lord's scorecard, which measured six by about ten inches – shades of Wilfred Rhodes aiming to pitch on a pocket handkerchief. Rockley's skills were reinforced by a keen appreciation of a batsman's strengths and weaknesses. He was adept at setting the right field for each opponent and many a batsman was lured into hitting the ball to the precise spot where a fielder had been positioned. He hardly ever pitched short. If Rockley was to be hit, a batsman had to be prepared to use his feet to get to the pitch of the ball and to correctly judge its pace and flight. Even then it was a risky business and the fact is that Rockley Wilson was rarely knocked off his length in any serious match. He did not mind conceding the odd boundary when it was part of his plan to get a wicket. In one county match at Bramall Lane, Frank Mann (a good friend of Rockley) hit him for two successive sixes into the bowling green alongside the pavilion. As Rockley would have it, the next ball was a little wider and a little higher and was skied to Waddington in the deep, exactly as the bowler had planned.[5] Exaggeration or not, Rockley's accuracy and guile are beyond question.

When it came to fielding, in his early years Rockley was a good close fielder, his best position being in the slips. And he was always an excellent fielder off his own bowling. But he had a weak throwing arm and was something of a liability if posted to the outfield. As we shall see this weakness was to bring him much distress when he played in Australia in 1920/21.

The three elder brothers were all competent cricketers but not in the same class as Clem and Rockley. The eldest, Reginald Thorp Wilson (always known as Rex) born in 1866, played for Cambridge Crusaders, effectively the University's Second XI, and for Sheffield Collegiate Cricket Club after he had established himself in the family solicitor practice in the town. He was President of Sheffield Collegiate from 1910 to 1953. Cyril Reynold Wilson was born in 1867. At Oxford he played for Exeter College but not for the University. He also became a solicitor in Sheffield and played for Sheffield Collegiate Cricket Club. He was a leg break bowler of a similar style to Rockley Wilson and in a long playing career he took many wickets for the club. His enthusiasm for cricket over many years made him the best known of the Wilson brothers in the Sheffield area. Cyril was a Vice-President of Sheffield Collegiate in the 1920s and served for 32 years on the Committee of the Yorkshire County Cricket Club. The third of the brothers, Rowland

---

5   Rockley took Mann's wicket eleven times in first-class cricket, more often than any other batsman who faced him.

Alwyn Wilson, was born in 1868. A medium-fast bowler, he played for Trinity College, Cambridge and for the University in three first-class matches but did not win a Blue – he was contemporary with the redoubtable Sam Woods. He played for various other clubs including Sheffield Collegiate, Old Rugbeians, Free Foresters, Butterflies and for Worcestershire before the county club achieved first-class status. Rowland Alwyn also entered the church and was ordained in 1894. Like his father, he ended his clerical career as a canon.

Clem and Rockley also played for Sheffield Collegiate in their younger days. At least once all five brothers were in the team. Rockley's first appearance for the club seems to have been in 1896, when he had a couple of five-wicket hauls. A photograph of the Sheffield Collegiate team against Hallam taken in 1897 or 1898 includes a youthful Rockley as well as his brothers R.A. and C.R.Wilson. While at Cambridge, and indeed for a few years afterwards, Rockley made occasional appearances for Sheffield Collegiate though not always with the success that might have been expected of such a talented cricketer. The report of a match in 1901 against Sheffield United comments "The visitors had the assistance of E.R.Wilson, next year's Cambridge captain, but in neither department of the game was he successful, his two wickets being secured at an expensive cost while he had about ten minutes batting in which he made 11." There were games when he justified his reputation, however. He scored 101 not out and took five for 38 against Shireoaks in 1906, for example.

Sheffield Collegiate Cricket Club was therefore an important part of the cricketing lives of the Wilson family. The Club was founded in 1881 by ex-pupils of the Sheffield Collegiate School. In its early years the club played many of its matches at Bramall Lane. In due course it acquired its own ground at Tinsley, Sheffield, and then entered sides in local cricket leagues. In 1919 Sheffield Collegiate moved to Abbeydale Park since when it has been a major force in league cricket in South Yorkshire.[6]

At a less serious level of cricket, in the 1880s Rex and Cyril, and occasionally one of the other brothers, played for Bolsterstone in

---

6   The writer has drawn on David Wilson's fascinating book, *A Century of the Sheffield Collegiate Cricket Club*, published privately in 1981. David Wilson was a prominent member of the Club after the Second World War. Rockley Wilson was the most celebrated cricketer to have played for Sheffield Collegiate until Michael Vaughan wrested that honour from him 100 years later.

The Sheffield Collegiate side which played Hallam in either 1897 or 1898.
Standing (l to r): Umpire Pring, F.Allan, G.Bott, F.Wood, Rev A.R.Wilson.
Seated: J.W.Aizlewood, J.M.Clayton, H.B.Willey, C.R.Wilson, Dr H.Lockwood.
On the ground: H.Willey, E.R.Wilson and "Joe".

matches against local club sides. More in the nature of social events, between 1885 and 1891 Rex Wilson raised invitation sides to play local teams and other invitation elevens in Bolsterstone. In 1891, a team entirely made up of Wilson family members, including Rockley, played an eleven of Smiths, with the Wilsons winning the two innings match by ten wickets.[7] There was even a Ladies against Gentlemen match at Middleton Hall, home of Cyril Wilson, where Rockley captained the Ladies XI – presumably because he was the youngest – and his four brothers played for the Gentlemen, who were required to bat with broomsticks but were still victorious.

Details of the cricketing lives of the Wilson brothers at least into the 1920s are documented in a number of scrapbooks of newspaper cuttings compiled by Clem and later, and less methodically, by Rockley. The scrapbooks contain scorecards of

---

7   There are suggestions that a repeat fixture took place in 1901 but no record of such a match has been unearthed.

games involving any of the Wilson brothers, whether social, club or first-class matches, and also newspaper reports of several of the first-class matches in which Clem and Rockley played.[8] Clem's scrapbooks of his trips to America in 1896 with an Oxford and Cambridge side and with Lord Hawke's side to South Africa in 1898/99 were donated to MCC by his son, the late David Wilson. The surviving scrapbooks of cuttings in the possession of David Wilson's family show what a remarkable amount of cricket the Wilson brothers played in careers which, taken together, stretched from the 1880s into the 1930s. They were assisted in this by personal circumstances – occupations and financial resources – that allowed them ample opportunities to engage in cricket, and also by the wide circle of acquaintances and contacts in the cricketing world which led, as we shall recount in the case of Rockley, to many invitations to play for clubs and sides up and down the country. To leaf through the scrapbooks, and a family album of photographs of Rockley, is to enjoy a glimpse of a long passed, more leisurely and more urbane age.

*Rockley Wilson
did not think of his bowling
as 'round-arm'.*

*This picture,
taken after the Great War,
seems to suggest otherwise.*

---

8   Sadly few of the cuttings show the year of the match and in later scrapbooks the cuttings are clearly not in date order, reducing somewhat their value as a statement of record.

Chapter Two
School and University

The Reverend Wilson was determined to provide the best possible education for his sons. Parents at the time had no compunction about sending their children, at any rate their sons, away to boarding school. The Wilsons' aim was to place the boys at one of the leading public schools, but their father endeavoured to arrange that no son should be at the same school at the same time. The two older Wilson boys, Rex and Cyril, attended Shrewsbury and Haileybury schools respectively and Rowland Alwyn went to Rugby. Uppingham was the chosen school for Clement. In Rockley's case, his father chose to send him to Bilton Grange School, a preparatory school near Rugby that prepared its pupils for senior school at 13 years, and in particular for Rugby School. Rockley's prep school was established in 1887, after the purchase of the Bilton Grange mansion by the Reverend Walter Earle, the school's first headmaster. In 1887 Rockley was already eight years old and it is likely that he attended the local school in Bolsterstone before being sent to Bilston Grange. It is rather surprising that Rockley's father should have chosen so untried an institution for the education of his youngest son in his formative years. Perhaps he was influenced by the boldness of the Reverend Earle's venture and the fact that the headmaster had previously been a housemaster at Uppingham School, where Rockley's brother Clem was proving an outstanding pupil.

*Rockley Wilson
at Bilston Grange School,
probably in 1891.*

We know little of the part that cricket played in the curriculum of Bilton Grange School. However, some coaching in the game was provided and Rockley must have taken part in matches at the school. Above is a charming photograph of a young Rockley, nonchalantly posed with a cricket bat, taken when he was a pupil at Bilton Grange. We know that Rockley impressed his headmaster with his talent. The Reverend Earle wrote to Rockley's father on his progress at school as a twelve-year-old: "You have a capital boy blessed with the happy way of doing everything right – and can't he play cricket too." It was at Bilton Grange that Rockley became fascinated with the history, personalities and statistics of the game, an interest that he was to maintain throughout his life.

It was not pre-ordained that Rockley would go on to Rugby School. In the same letter to Rockley's father, the headmaster says "Let us wait and see what happens at Rugby before ... we talk of Marlborough and Winchester." But in the event it was to be Rugby. Rockley was an able pupil. In 1892 he secured a place at Rugby by winning a Mathematics Scholarship at the school and coming fifth in the Classics Scholarship examination.

Under the firm leadership of its headmaster Dr John Percival, who had given up the presidency of Trinity College, Oxford, to return to schoolmastering, Rugby School was recovering the high reputation it had enjoyed a generation earlier when Thomas Arnold was headmaster. The daily routine for the boys was harsh, with cold baths and chapel before breakfast, and discipline was strict. The practice of fagging could be humiliating if not downright brutal. For Rockley, a shy and not particularly robust youngster, adjustment to life at the school could not have been easy. But like other public schools in the last half of the nineteenth century, Rugby set great store on the importance of sport, and particularly of cricket, in the education of its "young gentlemen."[9] Rockley Wilson excelled at most sports. He was an outstanding middle distance runner, winning the school mile competition in three successive years, his time of 4 minutes 46 seconds in 1898, the last of these, being the third fastest ever recorded at Rugby. Rockley also played rackets and fives to an excellent standard, and, though to a lesser standard, rugby.

---

9   In *Tom Brown's Schooldays*, the famous novel by Thomas Hughes set in Rugby School, when a master observes that cricket is a "noble game", Tom replies, "Isn't it. But it's more than a game. It's an institution."

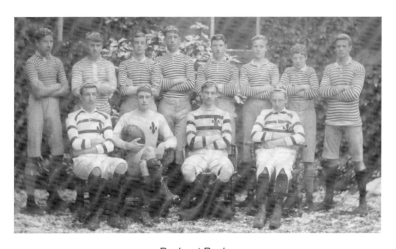

Rugby at Rugby.
Rockley Wilson, third from the left in the back row,
in W.G.Michel's House XV in wintry weather, 1896.

But it was at cricket that he particularly made his mark, benefiting from the coaching of Tom Emmett, the old Yorkshire fast bowler.[10] According to Rockley, Emmett "could bowl so well it was easy to imagine how good he must have been in his prime and he had a horrible ball which came with his arm in a most bewildering manner."[11] Cricket at Rugby was at a low ebb when Emmett was appointed coach in 1889, but his relaxed yet perceptive style of coaching soon led to an improvement. In Rockley's time Rugby played only one of the other leading public schools, Marlborough, in a fixture which dated from 1855: a second inter-school match against Clifton was only established in 1909. The public schools' varied fixture lists and the lack of regular matches between them made it difficult to assess their relative merits; among other sides that Rugby habitually played were a number of Oxford and Cambridge colleges, Free Foresters, Old Rugbeians, Rugby Town, Liverpool and MCC – who usually included at least a couple of county cricketers in their sides. However, W.J.Ford, in his annual review of public school cricket in *Wisden* rated Rugby among the top six school sides in all the years that Rockley was to play for the school.

---

10 Pelham (later, Sir Pelham) Warner was a pupil at Rugby School from 1888 until 1892, Rockley Wilsons's first year at the school. A chapter in his autobiography *Long Innings,* George G. Harrap and Company, 1951, describes Pelham Warner's own cricket experiences at the school. It was at Rugby that Pelham Warner came to be known as "Plum".
11 Interview in *Cricket,* 6 July, 1905.

Rockley's performances in 1895, the first of these, were not particularly eye-catching. The school magazine's verdict was "Did not do himself justice as a bat; a little too impatient to score; fair right hand slow bowler; a good field."[12] In 1896 he was more successful. In that season he was third in the batting averages with 24.86 from 14 innings and he topped the bowling averages with 28 wickets at 15.00. In the annual Rugby v Marlborough match at Lord's, Wilson had an outstanding game with the ball. Marlborough were beaten by an innings and 35 runs in a single day, Wilson taking three for 24 and six for 19 in the Marlborough innings. Recognition of his development into a fine all-round player, and a thinking cricketer, came with his election as captain of the "Light Blues" for the 1897 season.[13]

It was a very successful season for the young man, although he was out of action for a month with a broken finger sustained in the match against Balliol College in June. Rockley Wilson topped both the batting and the bowling averages with 460 runs at 51.11 and 31 wickets at 14.93. His batting average was boosted by an innings of 206 not out against New College, Oxford in May. The College were dismissed for 139. Opening the innings for Rugby, Wilson was joined at 39 for three wickets by W.G.Cobb. The pair then batted through to the close in an unbeaten stand of 308, with Cobb completing his own century in the process. "Wilson scored at a great pace off all the bowlers opposed to him, his cutting, leg-hitting and driving being all equally good."[14] In the match against Trinity College, Cambridge, Rockley scored 100 out of a score of 193 for four in a handsome Rugby victory over the university students. In the annual fixture with Marlborough in 1897 Rugby lost by three wickets but Wilson again had an outstanding match, this time with the ball, taking seven for 66 and three for 52. W.J.Ford, in his annual review for *Wisden* in 1898, remarked: "Wilson was

Rockley Wilson as captain of the Rugby School side, 1897.

---

12   *The Meteor*, 18 October, 1895, p.109.
13   Rugby's cricketers first wore duck egg blue shirts in 1843 and have continued to do so ever since.
14   *The Meteor*, 22 May, 1897, p.52.

a fine cricketer all-round, as patient with the bat as with the ball, and he certainly struck me as having a very old head on his shoulders when he tempted the Marlborough boys to their ruin with his curly slows." The school's assessment was that Wilson had proved "a thoroughly keen and good captain under whom a moderate team developed into a good one. Began the season with some really fine innings but latterly was handicapped by a broken finger. Slow right hand bowler with considerable command of the ball and knowledge of the game."[15] Clearly, Rockley Wilson was emerging as an accomplished batsman and highly promising slow bowler, and he was invited to play for privately raised sides in good class club cricket. In 1897, for example, he played for M.H.Marsden's XI during the Spalding Cricket Festival, taking six for 63 in Spalding's first innings, seven for 73 in their second, and scoring 73 out of 333 in the visitors' only innings. This match was a forerunner to the many, later in his career, that Rockley was to play for invitation elevens at cricket weeks and festivals up and down the country.

A point of interest is that Rockley's brother, the Reverend R.A.Wilson, appeared for the Free Foresters against Rugby School in each of Rockley's seasons in the First XI and on each occasion his bowling caused the schoolboys some difficulties. In the match in 1896, for example, R.A.Wilson took three for 31 and seven for 25 in the School's two innings: his dismissals included that of his brother for a stubborn 38 in Rugby's first innings. Rowland Alwyn had been a master at the school for a short time after he left Cambridge and before he entered the church. He had also helped with the organisation of cricket at the school.[16]

With his sporting prowess and a sense of humour that could border on the mischievous, it is not surprising that Rockley was very popular with his fellow pupils. A contemporary at Rugby observed "nothing in which he was concerned could ever be dull."[17] He was a keen member of the school Debating Society, revelling in the opportunities it provided for witticisms and welcoming the opportunity to propose radical motions. For

---

15   *The Meteor,* 12 October, 1897, p.109.
16   Pelham Warner is quite clear on the point in his autobiographies, *My Cricketing Life*, Holder and Stoughton, 1921, pp.44-46, which are an appreciation of Warner by R.A.Wilson, and *Long Innings*, op.cit., p.30. Curiously R.A.Wilson does not appear in Rugby's register of teachers, no doubt because his appointment was short-term.
17   Letter to *The Times*, 26 July, 1957, commenting on Rockley Wilson's obituary in *The Times* on 22 July, 1957.

example, he proposed the motion that women should be given the vote in Parliamentary elections: perhaps predictably, given the venue and the year, the motion was lost by 36 votes to 12. Rockley also unsuccessfully opposed the motion that sport was damaged by the increasing participation of professional players, arguing that professionalism was better than sham amateurism, "under which a man could find a mysterious five pound note in his boot after the match." Although Rockley confided in one of the school debates that he "was quite looking forward to an athletic career under academic auspices in the States," it was taken for granted by both school and family that Rockley would go up to Cambridge to continue his classical education. In the event Wilson did well enough scholastically for that purpose though, as one of his reports had it, he gave "two thoughts to cricket to every one to his work."

It was no surprise that Rockley Wilson was made Head of School for his final year and he expected to continue as cricket captain in his final season. But it was not to be. Rockley Wilson's final year at Rugby ended ignominiously. As cricket historian Anthony Woodhouse intriguingly put it, a "difference of opinion with authority caused E.R.Wilson to leave Rugby early"[18] and the consequence was that he played no cricket for the school in the 1898 season and the captaincy was handed to C.S.Hannay in his stead. The "difference of opinion" arose this way. Having been awarded the prize in a Latin competition for which he was unprepared, he admitted that he had submitted the (unsuccessful) entry of a previous student. Cheating could not be tolerated at Rugby School. Despite his prompt confession, though not formally expelled Rockley was required to leave the school forthwith. There was no public reference to the incident and its consequences. The school magazine had reported Rockley's appearances for the school cricket team over the previous three seasons in detail, and publicised his arrangements for net practice for the 1898 season, but from then on he might as well have ceased to exist.

We can be sure that his misdemeanour would have caused his parents much distress – it was said of his father that "he quietly boasted that he strictly adhered to the great truths of the Bible."[19] It is not surprising that, having left the school early, Rockley spent

---

18   Anthony Woodhouse, *A Who's Who of Yorkshire County Cricket Club*, Breedon Books, 1992, p.227.

19   *Hallamshire Worthies*, J.W.Northend, 1927, p.147.

most of the summer at Cambridge in lodgings with his brother Clem, who had gone up to Trinity College from Uppingham School in 1895 (and in 1898 was captain of the University side) rather than at home in Bolsterstone. We do not know how much cricket Rockley played that summer for other teams, but it seems very likely that he would have played some club cricket in the Cambridge area if not in his home village of Bolsterstone.

Cambridge University Years

Following the path of his father and his brothers Rowland Alwyn and Clement, Rockley entered Trinity College, Cambridge in the Michaelmas term of 1898. Rockley would surely have enjoyed his time at the University and the range of sporting, cultural and social activities that it offered. A serious illness had put paid to any ambitions in athletics, so it was upon his cricket that Rockley concentrated when at the University. Off the playing fields, it was at Cambridge that Rockley developed a passion for billiards at which he became a proficient player. When at home in Bolsterstone, he would have played at Broomhead Hall with his relation Reginald Henry Rimington-Wilson who was one of the outstanding amateur billiards players of his day. At school Rockley had also become fond of cards and at Cambridge he was an enthusiastic and skilful poker player. Once, at Cambridge, he took the bank at roulette with the cricket club's subscriptions that he had just collected – he was Secretary in 1901 – and doubled them. In these rather raffish interests, Rockley was perhaps kicking against the traces of his strict upbringing in a very religious household.

Academically Rockley did not do himself justice. There is no doubting his scholastic abilities, but he was inclined to idleness and found it hard to find time for his studies. He probably did not share the ambitions of most of his fellow students to use a Cambridge education as a springboard into the civil service, the learned professions or politics. When he graduated in 1901 in Classics it was only in the lower division of the Second Class. Probably, as was said of him at Rugby, Rockley treated his cricket more seriously than his studies. Certainly, his cricket career blossomed while he was at the University.

He did well in the Freshmen's match in 1899, scoring 60 runs and taking eight wickets and impressing the Cambridge captain

G.L.Jessop, but he was not included in the Cambridge side for the opening first-class match of the season against A.J.Webbe's XI. Yet this match was to be the occasion for Rockley Wilson's first-class debut. Of the visitors' party of twelve, two, F.G.J.Ford and C.P.Foley,[20] were unable to play on the day, and Rockley was asked to appear as a "make-up" (substitute) against his own University. Although A.J.Webbe's XI included such celebrated players as K.S.Ranjitsinhji, J.T.Hearne and F.W.Tate, it was weakened in the course of the first day initially when Webbe dropped out at the luncheon interval, to be replaced by John Daniell, a second year Cambridge undergraduate; and then when Hylton Philipson, the wicketkeeper, was injured and replaced by W.P.Robertson, a Cambridge freshman also, like Rockley Wilson, playing his first first-class match. Nonetheless, Cambridge's victory by an innings and 62 runs was a notable one. T.L.Taylor, who had a wonderful career at Uppingham School where he was a contemporary of C.E.M.Wilson, scored 90 and Gilbert Jessop, the captain, 60 in Cambridge's 464. A.J.Webbe's XI made 224 in their first innings: Wilson, batting at No.3, scored 117 not out, despite being up until 3 am the night before playing poker, and Ranji only 17. Overnight rain made the wicket treacherous for the final day. Dismissed for a duck, Ranji remarked "Filthy wicket. No one will get 20 on it."[21] Not to be disheartened, Wilson, opening the innings this time, scored 70 out of A.J.Webbe's team's 178 which *Wisden* described as "a remarkable effort."

Five days later Wilson made his debut for the University against Yorkshire, also at Fenner's.[22] This time the visitors won by an innings. Gilbert Jessop, in explosive form, scored 171 not out out of Cambridge's first innings of 246. Rockley Wilson was next top scorer with 24. In reply, Yorkshire amassed 429 with centuries from Jack Brown and F.S.Jackson. Wilson took three for 103 off 34 overs. His victims in a marathon spell of economical bowling were Jackson, George Hirst and Wilfred Rhodes, a celebrated trio indeed. In the second innings Cambridge totalled 100 of which Wilson scored 12. Despite this heavy defeat, Rockley Wilson could take considerable satisfaction from the two matches in which,

---

20 Foley played instead for MCC against Lancashire at Lord's.

21 W.F.Ford, *A History of the Cambridge University Cricket Club: 1820-1921*, Wm. Blackwood, 1902, p.147.

22 He replaced A.E.Fernie, who had played in the match against Webbe's side. Fernie was a slow left-arm bowler who played 21 matches for Cambridge over four seasons, winning Blues in 1897 and 1900. He also played Minor Counties cricket for Staffordshire and Berkshire.

probably uniquely, he had played against and for his University. From this point on, his place in the Cambridge First XI was assured, and he could also be sure that this early demonstration of his considerable promise had been noted in the county of his birth. In fact soon after the end of the University's season, Rockley Wilson was to make his debut for Yorkshire, again following in the footsteps of his brother Clem who had first played for the county in 1896.

For Cambridge, Rockley appeared in eight first-class games in 1899 including two matches against MCC, a match against the touring Australians, which the visitors won convincingly by ten wickets, and the drawn match against Oxford in which he got his Blue. He batted well up the order, often opening the innings, but after his impressive performance for A.J.Webbe's XI, his batting disappointed. He scored 307 runs in total, averaging 19.18 with a best score of 49 against MCC at Lord's, in his first appearance in a first-class match at cricket's headquarters. As the season wore on, his captain made more use of Rockley Wilson's bowling and he finished with 30 wickets at 26.86, more wickets than any other Cambridge bowler, but rather expensive by later Rockley

The Cambridge University side in Rockley Wilson's freshman year, 1899.
Standing (l to r): A.E.Hind, L.J.Moon, E.F.Penn, J.Daniell.
Seated: G.E.Winter, T.L.Taylor, G.L.Jessop (captain), J.N.Stogdon,
H.H.B.Hawkins.
On the ground: S.H.Day, E.R.Wilson.

standards. Certainly it was his batting rather than his bowling that caught *Wisden*'s eye. In its review of Cambridge's season, *Wisden* observed: "For E.R.Wilson it is quite safe to predict an excellent future. A young batsman who plays so perfectly straight and possesses such defence and patience is bound to do well."

In July 1899, after his first year as an undergraduate and with only nine first-class matches behind him, Rockley Wilson had the immense satisfaction of being chosen to play for Yorkshire in the Championship match against Somerset at Hull. It was not unusual of course for talented cricketers at the ancient universities to appear for county sides at this time and the powers-that-be at Yorkshire would have been well aware of Wilson's potential. But it was a rapid rise. The opportunity to blood the young undergraduate arose because a number of Yorkshire's regular side were involved in the Gentlemen v Players match at Lord's, namely F.S.Jackson for the Gentlemen and J.T.Brown, George Hirst and Wilfred Rhodes for the Players. Rockley's pleasure would have been increased by the fact that Clem was also selected – it is a rare occurrence for brothers to appear in a Yorkshire side in a Championship match – but Clem damaged his hand when fielding soon after Somerset began their innings and the Somerset captain agreed that he could be replaced by Yorkshire's twelfth man, T.H.Hirst. Batting at No.4, Rockley Wilson scored 55 in Yorkshire's first innings, figuring in a useful stand with Denton, but he was dismissed for a duck in the second innings. He bowled competently in both innings taking one for 39 off 16 overs in Somerset's first innings and two for 11 off 14 overs in the second. The match was drawn, a ferocious thunderstorm ending play prematurely with Yorkshire in sight of victory.

There was momentary embarrassment for Rockley at the start of his Yorkshire career. On opening his cricket bag in the Yorkshire dressing room, he uncovered a number of items of female underwear, put there by team-mates after a previous country house match near Liverpool. Lord Hawke, in his patrician way, remarked, "By Gad, you're a pretty brisk fellow", which in the sense intended, Rockley certainly was not.[23]

---

23   Presumably distaste for his feminine-sounding first name explains why E.R.Wilson was always known as Rockley. He once received a summons to report for jury service addressed to Miss Evelyn R.Wilson, containing the note "If you are in an advanced state of pregnancy or suffering from any other feminine ailment, you may apply for an exemption", which he had framed and hung in his house.

After his quite promising start at Hull, Rockley played in three other matches for Yorkshire that summer each time when, for one reason or another, Stanley Jackson was not available. In the matches against Leicestershire and Hampshire he opened the innings with John Tunnicliffe. Clearly it was his batting rather than his bowling which had impressed the county at this time. His performances bore this out. In his four matches he averaged 31.00 with the bat, top score 79 against Warwickshire, when he and George Hirst put on 128 for the fifth wicket, and took four wickets at 32.50, and one catch. *Wisden* predicted cautiously that Wilson and his fellow undergraduate T.L.Taylor "may render valuable service to Yorkshire in the near future."

Taking the season as a whole, Rockley Wilson scored 649 runs at 29.50 and took 36 wickets at 27.44. These were quite promising figures but young Rockley Wilson could have had no illusions about his chances of winning a regular place in the Yorkshire side while he continued his University studies. Although Yorkshire just failed to win the Championship in 1899, at full strength they were a powerful side on the verge of a decade of unprecedented success. The county had a strong pool of players to call upon if their regulars were not available, or to give the professionals some respite from the rigours of full-time cricket. Among the amateurs they could draft into the side was Ernest Smith, a graduate of Oxford, a dashing bat and a quick bowler who, between 1888 and 1907, was regularly brought into the side in the latter half of the season – a role that Rockley Wilson was to play later in his own career. Then there was T.L.Taylor, Rockley Wilson's Cambridge contemporary and clearly a better batsman, who also made his debut for the county in 1899 and thereafter established himself in the side until the end of the 1902, when he chose to concentrate on his business career. Frank Mitchell, another Cambridge man, first played regularly for Yorkshire in 1899, and then, like Stanley Jackson, volunteered to serve in South Africa in the Boer War and missed the 1900 season.[24] He returned and had a superb season in 1901 and then left to settle in South Africa. And there were others.

No doubt Rockley Wilson's attitude was that the future could be left to look after itself. As it turned out, the 1900 season was a very full one for the young man. He played in all eleven of Cambridge's first-class matches, starting on 7 May with the annual season-

---

24   Frank Milligan, another Yorkshire cricketer who volunteered to fight in South Africa, died of his wounds in March, 1900.

raiser against A.J.Webbe's XI, and four matches for Yorkshire, the last against Essex at Harrogate starting on 2 August. For Cambridge, after a slow start to the season, he scored 569 runs at 29.94, placing him third in the University's batting averages. His highest score was 82 against Sussex at Hove and the next 80 against Surrey at Fenner's. He took 21 wickets for Cambridge at 26.76, with one quite outstanding performance of seven for 79 against MCC at Lord's. He also had the satisfaction of dismissing W.G. in the return fixture against London County at Crystal Palace. While Grace was in the twilight of his career, it can be pointed out that he had made his final Test appearance for England only in the previous season. Rockley's satisfaction at his dismissal would have been increased had he known that W.G.'s opinion of him, on first seeing Wilson bowl, was "Well! Of all the bad bowlers I've ever seen, this fellow is the very worst." In the high-scoring drawn match against Oxford University, Wilson batted competently, scoring 45 and 23 not out in Cambridge's two innings, but he failed to take a single Oxford wicket. Reviewing the Cambridge season, *Wisden* referred to Wilson as a "capital" batsman but added cuttingly that as a bowler he "could not inspire batsmen with the least feeling of apprehension." The Press could also be scathing of his bowling in his early years at Cambridge. The *Evening News*, for example, reported that "Wilson serves up a slow, tired-looking sort of ball."[25] Rockley was to show that these were premature judgements. His slow right-arm bowling was to prove increasingly effective as he gained experience against top-class batsmen.

This experience continued in four matches for Yorkshire where the absence of Stanley Jackson and Frank Mitchell provided a further opportunity. But Rockley did not make good use of his chance. He scored only 63 runs, 41 of them in one innings against Nottinghamshire and was rarely bowled, taking only four wickets, albeit at a miserly 6.75. He had been injured during the second match, against Worcestershire, and then had to miss a few games, but this was hardly an excuse. Taking the season as a whole he scored 632 runs at 27.47 and took 25 wickets at 23.56. These were respectable figures, but after his disappointing performances for Yorkshire, it was not surprising that the county did not call upon him in 1901.

---

25   Interview in *Cricket*, 6 July, 1905, p.242, also the source for the remark by
      W.G.Grace.

This photograph is believed to show Rockley Wilson bowling in one of his four Varsity matches at Lord's.

Before the 1901 cricket season was upon him, Rockley had to prepare for his examinations for his degree at the end of the Easter term. Once examinations were over – as we have noted he did not achieve a particularly distinguished degree – he was able to give his full attention to cricket. The 1901 season was a poor one for the University, with only one victory, against Worcestershire. The main reason was the limited Cambridge bowling. The captain, F.P.Knox, had to rely heavily on his two slow bowlers, the left-arm spinner E.M.Dowson and Rockley Wilson. It was in this season that Rockley began to show his real worth as a bowler. Dowson took the most wickets, but Rockley topped the bowling averages with 37 wickets at 24.78. His outstanding performance was against Worcestershire when he took seven for 37 and seven for 38. Moreover, he had the satisfaction of dismissing W.G.Grace twice during the season, against London County at Fenner's when the Old Man was bowled and later, at Lord's, when Rockley had him caught. He had his off days, however; he conceded 182 runs off 43 overs for a single wicket against the South Africans, who won by an innings and 215 runs, and none for 129 off 39 overs against Sussex at Hove. But these were exceptions. With the bat, Wilson scored 469 runs at an average of 31.26, making him third in the University's batting averages.

Rockley Wilson's outstanding performance in 1901 was in the University match at Lord's, which again was drawn. He scored 118 out of Cambridge's first innings total of 325. Opening the batting for Cambridge before a crowd of some 19,000, on a pitch that after overnight rain assisted the bowlers, Rockley batted with much circumspection. Indeed he scored only eleven runs in his second hour at the crease and only four while Dowson was scoring 38, though later in his innings he did become more adventurous. He was seventh out when he unluckily played on off his pads to R.A. Williams after four hours at the crease. Rockley followed his marathon innings by taking five wickets for 71 off no fewer than 45 overs in Oxford's first innings, a considerable feat of stamina as well as of skill. The match could well have been won by Cambridge for when Oxford were 149 runs behind in their second innings with only three wickets to fall, F.H. Hollins edged a ball into the slips where Rockley caught it "three or four inches from the ground" (in his words) only for the batsman to be given not out as both umpires were unsighted. Not for nothing did *Wisden* say "he was quite the hero of the match", and *The Times* that "he stood pre-eminent." As Rockley's brother Clem had scored a century for Cambridge against Oxford in 1898, this was only the second time that brothers had scored centuries in the University match, the previous pair being H.K.Foster in 1895 and R.E.Foster in 1900. A hundred at Lord's was a splendid finale to his season of first-class

This cartoon of 1901 has "Lord Yawkshire" saying "Hm, very good - but I haven't a vacancy just now. I-er-almost wish I had."

Wilson's batting in the Varsity match of 1901 advanced his case for selection by Yorkshire: he did not, however, play for the county in that year.

"TO HIM THAT HATH."

LORD YAWKSHIRE — "H'm, yes—very good—but I haven't a vacancy just now. I—'er—almost wish I had."

cricket. His innings was widely praised in the national Press and increased the reputation he was building in his native county.

Rockley gave up his rooms in Trinity College after graduation, but decided to stay on at Cambridge to accept the honour of captaining the University in the 1902 season, once again following in the footsteps of his brother Clem. He had decided to make his career in school teaching and his plan was to take up a suitable appointment after the 1902 cricket season. He also planned to spend some weeks in the close season in France, improving his command of spoken French. But any immediate thoughts of France were put out of his mind by an invitation to tour America and Canada in September and October, 1901 with a team captained by B.J.T.Bosanquet. As well as the excitement of a visit to the New World, and in particular the city of Philadelphia, with its unique place in American history and its cricketing traditions, the tour was a great opportunity to continue his development as a cricketer.

Tour of North America

The tour party consisted of twelve amateur cricketers – and included two players who later became knights of the realm and one a clerk in holy orders. Bernard Bosanquet had played for Oxford University and Middlesex in the preceding three seasons and was to become one of cricket's immortals as the inventor of the googly. In a memoir, Bosanquet explained how he perfected the googly using a tennis ball on a billiard table and that he first bowled a googly in 1900 in a match against Leicestershire. But his innovation was not taken seriously in England; it was two or three years later that googly bowling became a regular feature of the cricket scene. Even though he followed the game closely, it seems unlikely that Rockley Wilson was aware of this development in the art of spin bowling when he accepted the invitation to tour. Rockley was a finger spinner but we can be sure that as the tour progressed he would have been interested to learn about the wicket-taking potential of the new weapon in the wrist spinner's armoury.[26]

Cricket had been played in America since colonial days, but it was in the nineteenth century that its popularity grew until, as the

---

26   Another player in the party who later was to become an exponent of googly bowling was Reggie Schwarz who had also played for Middlesex in 1901.

century wore on, it came increasingly to be challenged by the appeal of the less leisurely baseball. In 1844 a cricket match between teams from the United States and Canada became the first international sporting event in the modern world. By the middle of the century Philadelphia had become the leading centre for cricket though it was also played in other places including New York, Boston, Baltimore, Chicago and Pittsburgh. Haverford College, ten miles from Philadelphia, founded in 1833 by Quakers and one of North America's leading liberal arts colleges, became a nursery of many great American players. (When the College had toured England in 1896, Rockley Wilson had played against them for Rugby School.) The College and the club sides in Philadelphia, often coached by English professionals, thrived. In the sport's heyday there were more than one hundred cricket clubs in the area. From the ranks of the local clubs, the Gentlemen of Philadelphia teams were selected. There were cup and league competitions and an annual Gentlemen v Players fixture. Tours to England were organised. From 1870 onwards there were frequent tours of North America by teams from England and Australia and West Indies. The cricket was of such a standard that there was serious talk of Test matches being played one day.[27]

The first match of Bosanquet's tourists was against Eighteen Philadelphia Colts on 20, 21 and 23 September, 1901 and the final one against an Eleven of Canada in Toronto on 11 and 12 October. In between a twelve-a-side match was played against the Knickerbocker Athletic Club of Bayonne, New Jersey and two matches against the Gentlemen of Philadelphia. These latter were the matches that mattered both to the team and in terms of the development of Rockley Wilson's career. The tour was not a success and for Rockley it was a very great disappointment. The tourists won three and lost two of their matches. In all matches, Wilson scored only 67 runs, top score 37, at an average of 8.37. With the ball, he took only 14 wickets at an average of 15.71. Of the two first-class matches against the Gentlemen of Philadelphia, the tourists won the first game by 61 runs but were soundly beaten by 229 runs in the second. Wilson's performances were wretched. Opening the innings in both matches, his scores were two, nine, seven and nine, an average of 6.75. He also had limited success

---

27   The writer has drawn on Rowland Bowen, *Cricket: A History of its Growth and Development throughout the World*, Eyre & Spottiswoode, 1970, for information on cricket in America at this time: likewise, later, for information on cricket in the West Indies and Argentina.

with the ball, though he did take five wickets in the Gentlemen's first innings of the second match (when they totalled 312, by far the highest innings score of either side on the tour), but at a cost of 100 runs from 17.3 six-ball overs. His final tally in the two games was eight wickets at 19.00.

At this distance in time it is impossible to account for Wilson's lack of success, especially after a satisfactory season in 1901 for Cambridge. He was young and inexperienced and would have found the playing conditions and surroundings unfamiliar. But he was not alone in that of course. The tour involved much travelling but at a leisurely pace and on some trips at least in some comfort. Rockley was never physically strong but fatigue hardly seems an explanation. Nor does it seem likely, given his background and personality, that Rockley would have been in anyway overawed by the occasion or by his team-mates, most of whom, like himself, had only limited first-class experience. Subsequently V.F.S. Crawford had a reasonably lengthy and successful career with Surrey and Leicestershire, but he also had little success on the tour. Only two of the party (other than Rockley) were to play Test cricket, Bosanquet and Frank Mitchell, the Yorkshireman who played two Tests for England and three for South Africa. Bosanquet finished top of the batting averages and second in the bowling. Mitchell, second in the batting averages, left the tour before the final match to begin the long journey back to South Africa. It is hard to imagine that Wilson felt out of place in the company of these players. Whatever the reasons for his disappointing performance, we can be sure that Rockley would not turn down any chance to make amends. As it happened just such an opportunity was soon to present itself.

Tour of West Indies

Hardly had Rockley had time to contemplate a winter spent at home in Bolsterstone, no doubt waiting impatiently for the start of the 1902 season, when he was invited to participate in a second overseas tour, this time to the West Indies with a party of University cricketers captained by R.A.Bennett, who played a few matches for Hampshire between 1896 and 1899. The party was to sail from Southampton immediately after the New Year and would barely be back in England before the start of the domestic season. To Rockley Wilson the tour would have appeared a heaven-sent opportunity to see more of the world and its different cultures and to continue his cricketing education. The first first-class match in the Caribbean had been in 1865, the first inter-colonial tournament in 1891 after which West Indian cricket developed rapidly. The first tour of the West Indies had been in 1895 and the first West Indies tour to England in 1900.

Bennett's party was not as strong as the one with which Rockley toured America. Almost all the players were under 30, "young blades" mostly from wealthy backgrounds. Only six of the party had played a full season of English cricket: there were only three regular bowlers, Bosanquet, E.M.Dowson and Wilson, and there was no depth to the batting. The side took their own umpire, A.A.White, at 31 one of the younger umpires in English first-class cricket: he had, though, umpired in the West Indies before, with A.A.Priestley's touring side of 1897. The tour was a long and arduous one, involving some 2,800 miles of travel by steamship between venues, on top of the 3,800 miles outward journey. The tourists played no fewer than 19 matches between 22 January and 9 April, 1902 of which 13 were won, five lost and one drawn. Thirteen of the matches were of first-class standard, namely two against each of Barbados, Jamaica, Trinidad and British Guiana and three matches against Combined West Indies XIs. The West Indies won this "series" by two matches to one.

Immediately on arriving in the West Indies Rockley received the news that his mother had died in Bolsterstone. There was of course no way in which a touring cricketer could return home in such circumstances. Not surprisingly Wilson stood down for the first match of the tour, with J.A.Davenport, an Army officer, being co-opted into the eleven as not all the side had arrived in Barbados. (Davenport scored two ducks, did not bowl and did not take a catch.) But after this sad beginning, and despite finding the climate decidedly uncomfortable, the tour was more successful for Rockley than his earlier trip to North America. Playing in 18 of the 19 matches, he scored 446 runs, with a highest score of 81, at an average of 20.27, and topped the bowling averages with 78 wickets at 10.37. In the first-class matches, Wilson scored 402 runs at an average of 25.12 and took 67 wickets at 11.44, conceding only 1.84 runs per six-ball over. His best performance came in the third match against the Combined West Indies XI, at Georgetown, British Guiana, which the visitors won by an innings and 330 runs. Wilson did not trouble the scorers in his innings, but had an outstanding match with the ball taking seven for 46 and seven for 16 in the

West Indies' innings. The latter was to prove the best bowling figures that Rockley produced in first-class cricket.[28] *Wisden* commented on the "peculiarities of the wickets" but even taking account of the assistance they might have provided, Wilson could justifiably feel that his reputation as a bowler had been enhanced by his three months' sojourn in the Caribbean.

---

28   This was an unusual match in several respects. The acting captain of Bennett's side, A.D.Whatman, won the toss and put the West Indies in to bat on a wet pitch, dismissing them for 92, with Wilson taking 7 for 46. Bennett's XI then scored 455, giving them a first innings lead of 363. In their second innings, West Indies were 13-0 at the end of the second day's play, on Saturday. When play resumed on Monday after overnight rain, Wilson and his Trinity College colleague, E.M.Dowson, bowling to a much changed batting order, took all ten wickets for only 20 runs in about twenty overs. Bennett's side thus won by an innings and 330 runs, still the largest innings win margin ever achieved in first-class cricket in the West Indies. Immediately after that match was over, Bennett's XI started a new first-class match at 3.15pm, this time against British Guiana. Whatman lost the toss this time and with the pitch still wet, Bennett's XI were sent in to bat and dismissed in just over two hours for 90, before play ended for the day.

Chapter Three
After Graduation

There was little time after Rockley had returned from the tour to assess the resources he would have at Cambridge for the 1902 season. Following the drawn matches in the three previous years, his main ambition as captain was to beat Oxford, a feat which his brother Clem had not achieved in his year as captain. He knew that he would be handicapped by the limitations of his bowling attack which, as in 1901, was heavily dependent on E.M.Dowson and himself. He pointed up this problem in a controversial way in a trial match at the beginning of the season. Captaining the First Twelve against the Next Sixteen in a trial match, he took fourteen for 73 in the Next's second innings. There was criticism that he had bowled himself so much, but his reason was that the bowling he had at his disposal in the Best Twelve was so weak that he had to bowl to make the trial match of any value. Events were to justify his view and the incident showed the imagination that Rockley could bring to his captaincy.

Of the eleven first-class matches that Cambridge played that season, four were won, four lost and three drawn. The summer of 1902 was exceptionally wet and a number of Cambridge's fixtures early in the season were ruined by rain. Had the weather been better there is no doubt that the University's results would have been impressive. Among Cambridge's victories was a splendid win against Surrey at The Oval. The University would in all probability have beaten them in the match at Fenner's earlier in the season had rain not brought the match to a premature close with Surrey following on in their second innings, having been shot out in the first for 92 with Wilson taking four for 53 and Dowson six for 33. A powerful Australian side beat the University by an innings and 183 runs with Victor Trumper scoring 128 out of Australia's 337.[29] Although Rockley Wilson took some punishment in this match, finishing with 4 for 107 off 38 overs, he would surely have admired

---

29   This innings was the highest of eleven centuries scored by Trumper in the 1902 season, showing that, once past the hundred mark, he was often ready to make way for a team-mate.

the glorious strokeplay of one of the finest batsmen of cricket's Golden Age. Rockley had a more satisfying match against London County at Crystal Palace. Not only did Cambridge win by five wickets with Rockley taking four for 15 off nine overs and four for 19 off 15 overs, he captured W.G.Grace's wicket in both innings. Rockley Wilson had now taken Grace's wicket five times in first-class matches, an achievement of which he was extremely proud. In later years, the feat was marked by the initials W.G. on the door of the toilet at his Winchester residence.

Between a rock and a hard place.
Rockley wedged between Billy Murdoch and W.G.Grace for the match between London County and Cambridge University at Crystal Palace in June, 1902.
Back row (l to r): E.F.Penn, J.Gilman, C.H.M.Ebden, C.E.Winter, P.R.May, J.H.Board, H.V.Hesketh-Prichard, L.Walker, W.Smith, A.E.Lawton, W.A.J.West (umpire).
Middle row: R.N.R.Blaker, W.L.Murdoch, E.R.Wilson, W.G.Grace, E.M.Dowson, L.O.S.Poidevin, L.V.Harper, T.Mycroft (umpire).
Front row: S.H.Day, F.B.Wilson, C.B.Llewellyn, G.Howard-Smith, R.M.Bell.

Rockley Wilson's captaincy led to controversy in the match against MCC at Lord's that immediately preceded the University match. MCC scored 607 in their first innings, the first three batsmen, P.F.Warner, C.J.Burnup and J.R.Mason, all getting centuries, but this was in large part because Wilson chose to experiment with his bowlers in an effort to find some effective alternatives to himself and E.M.Dowson. The University were then dismissed for 190, with Wilson failing to score, and in their second innings for 271, leaving

Cambridge 146 runs short of avoiding an innings defeat. But in Cambridge's second innings Wilson scored 142 in an innings lasting three and a half hours and in which he only just failed to carry his bat. This was to prove the highest score of Rockley Wilson's first-class career.

When it came to the University match, Rockley had the great satisfaction of captaining Cambridge to victory by five wickets. Oxford scored 206 and 251 in their two innings, Cambridge 186 and 274 for five wickets. A major factor in the success was the bowling of Rockley Wilson and Dowson. Opening the bowling in both Oxford innings, they took all but two of the twenty Oxford wickets, Rockley finishing with five for 53 off 35 overs and three for 66 off 26.5 overs. Dowson took ten wickets in the match and S.H.Day, who scored 117 not out in Cambridge's second innings and probably would have won the "Man of the Match" award had there been such a thing in those days, paid tribute to Wilson's captaincy. "He could make Dowson bowl without trying too many

Effortless superiority.
The Cambridge University side of 1902.
Standing (l to r): R.N.R.Blaker, C.E.Winter, L.T.Driffield, J.Gilman, F.B.Wilson.
Seated: S.H.Day, E.M.Dowson, E.R.Wilson (captain), L.V.Harper, E.F.Penn.
On the ground: C.M.H.Ebden.

tricks," he said.[30] Rockley Wilson was not only an exponent of the art of slow bowling, he had the knack of bringing out the best in any other slow bowler in his side.

To sum up his final season for Cambridge, Rockley had a rather patchy summer with the bat but was very effective with the ball. Despite the boost of his century against MCC, he averaged only 19.94 from 20 innings. Although Dowson took more wickets, Wilson topped the bowling averages with 54 wickets at a more economical return of 16.51. Aside from the statistics, Rockley Wilson could relish the fact that he and his brother Clem achieved the then unprecedented feat of appearing for Cambridge in eight successive seasons, Clem from 1895 until 1898 and Rockley from 1899 until 1902, of both captaining the side in his final year – though only in Rockley's case to victory – and of both recording centuries against Oxford. Between them, the brothers captured thirty one Oxford wickets at Lord's.

Each brother had graduated in the academic year before the year of his captaincy and it might be wondered on what grounds they were permitted to continue to appear for the University, let alone to captain the side. In years gone by some men had played for their University for several years after graduating and this led to pressure to clarify the rules on eligibility. Various proposals and rules were put forward, until in 1865 the matter was settled by the adoption of the following qualification rule: "That a man whose name is on the College books be qualified to play in the annual match between Oxford and Cambridge for the four consecutive years dating from the beginning of his first term of residence and those years only." The four year rule allowed graduates who had "gone down", but were not fully engaged in employment, to play for a fourth year though not in residence at the University. The rule also equalised the position between Oxford and Cambridge, as some Oxford students needed four years to graduate.[31] Hence Rockley Wilson was able to continue to play for Cambridge, and to captain the side, after he had graduated and left college.

Rockley Wilson's season of first-class cricket had not finished with the end of the University year. There were several matches still to be played in the County Championship and Rockley was selected

---

30 G.Chesterton and H.Doggart, *Oxford and Cambridge Cricket*, Willow Books, 1989, p.132.
31 *A History of the Cambridge University Cricket Club, 1820-1901*, op.cit., pp.14-15.

for one of these, against Worcestershire when he scored 63 runs in the first innings, but took no wickets in a rain-affected match. Any disappointment in not appearing more often was allayed by his selection for two matches at the Scarborough Cricket Festival in September, for MCC against Yorkshire and for the Gentlemen against the Players.

The MCC side, captained by W.Findlay of Oxford, who later was to become Secretary of MCC, was not a particularly strong one to take on the County Champions at full strength. But Yorkshire were beaten by 26 runs in two days in a low scoring match. The outstanding performance was that of Somerset's L.C.Braund, one of three England-capped players in MCC's team, who took six for 77 and six for 34 in the two Yorkshire innings with his leg-breaks, and top scored in MCC's first innings. Rockley was not invited to bowl at any stage of the match but he did make a most useful 24 runs, batting at No.5 in MCC's second innings of 100.

Rockley probably regarded his selection for the Gentlemen against the Players as the greater honour. The first-class game had expanded considerably since the first Gentlemen v Players match at Lord's in 1806, but the fixture was still a prestigious one. Scarborough had first hosted the fixture in 1885, when the Gentlemen won by an innings and 35 runs, W.G.Grace scoring 174 out of a total of 263 on a treacherous wicket. After the turn of the century, Scarborough became a regular venue along with Lord's and The Oval for the three Gentlemen v Players matches in the season.[32] The match at Lord's was clearly the outstanding fixture of the three and Pelham Warner considered that Rockley Wilson was one of the three best amateurs in his own time never to have played for the Gentlemen at Lord's. However, the status of the matches at the other two grounds was perhaps diluted by the practice of choosing a preponderance of southern players for the match at The Oval, and of northerners for that at Scarborough. Thus in the 1902 match at Scarborough, the Players included seven Yorkshiremen, including George Hirst as captain. The Gentlemen were captained by Lord Hawke and included F.S.Jackson, T.L.Taylor and E.Smith as well as Rockley Wilson.[33] Although

32   It continued to be so until 1962, when the distinction between amateurs and professionals in English first-class cricket was abolished and the fixture discontinued. Of the 39 matches played at Scarborough, the Players won 13, the Gentlemen won five and 19 were drawn.

33   Emphasising the class distinction in the venerable fixture, those appearing for the Gentlemen were accommodated in the Grand Hotel, and it was grand in Edwardian times, while the Players team had to find lodgings in the town.

J.M.Kilburn described the Scarborough Festival as "first-class cricket on holiday"[34], we can be sure that a match including so many Yorkshiremen would be hard-fought. The match was drawn, the Players scoring 314 and 259 for eight declared, the Gentlemen 363 (Taylor 102) and 133 for seven. Wilson scored five in his only innings and took four wickets in all, three of them for 94 off 27 overs in the Players' second innings. It could be described as a modest performance on his first appearance in a representative match in England.

---

34   J.M.Kilburn, *The Scarborough Cricket Festival*, Scarborough Cricket Club, 1948, p.11.

Chapter Four

A Singular Man

We will pause at this point in the story of Rockley Wilson's cricket career to say more about Rockley the man. He was a sensitive, modest and courteous person and, throughout his life, mildly eccentric. We have commented on Rockley's sense of humour and fun in the account of his school days. He carried these qualities into adulthood. Something of a gadfly, like many humorists he was not averse to taking a chance with authority, as the cheating incident at Rugby and some of his antics as a schoolmaster at Winchester illustrate. He was a natural raconteur and a master of the impromptu remark or aside. He spoke very softly, almost apologetically, in a high-pitched voice, leaning forward slightly, constantly fingering his tie. He had a slight speech impediment which led him to say "ve" rather than "the". His remarks, frequently laced with cricketing metaphors, were punctuated by a frequent "ta-ha" and he developed the habit of always repeating his punch-line.

Rockley would say, of people he did not like, "He is not a very nice man really, really." His more acerbic witticisms were directed at those whom he found discourteous or pompous. The best known of all Rockley Wilson anecdotes relates how, when talking to friends in the Long Room at Lord's, he greeted Lord Harris who offered a limp handshake and passed curtly on. Rockley, who was not popular with the Lord's 'establishment' at the time, for reasons that we shall come to in due course, muttered under his breath "Lucky to get a touch really, lucky to get a touch." Another well-known story has him murmuring, "A pleasure," as a woman for whom he was holding open a door at Harrods swept past without a word, and then pursuing her down the street to remark "And it would have been an even greater pleasure, madam, if you had said thank you." It was said of him that he was equally capable of snubbing a bishop and soothing a fretful baby. If really annoyed, Rockley could show quick bursts of temper. Obvious fools he did not suffer gladly.

Rockley Wilson was a keen and discerning collector of cricket books, ceramics, paintings, prints and other cricketana, as to a lesser extent was his brother Clem. Rockley always regretted that he had not started collecting earlier than he did and the limited funds he could devote to his collection was always a constraint. For example, in 1931 he was not able to meet the £500 asking price for the Ashley Cooper collection. Nevertheless, by judicious purchasing, over the years Rockley built up one of the finest cricket collections and libraries, particularly of prints and of the early literature of the game. A number of items in Rockley's collection were acquired on his overseas cricket tours. A catalogue of his collection of paintings, drawings and prints that Rockley made in 1934 survives. It contains details of nine oil paintings, thirteen drawings and ninety seven prints.[35] Rockley would of course have added to his collection after 1934. By his will, Rockley gave MCC the choice of any items in his collection (which even at the time of his death in 1957 must have been worth a very considerable sum) that they wished to have. All his paintings and drawings, many prints, some books and nearly all the glass and ceramic items were selected for MCC's collection. A further indication of the size and breadth of the collection from which Lord's has benefited is a letter of 30 November, 1987 to David Wilson from Stephen Green, the Lord's curator, that lists glass and ceramic items from the collection held by Lord's along with a variety of other cricket collectibles such as snuff and tobacco boxes, brass and metal ware and figures, commemorative handkerchiefs, presentation cricket balls and the like. The list runs to two foolscap pages. The rest of Rockley's collection, other than some items retained by the family, was sold commercially. Rockley would have been pleased that at least some of the prized items in his collection of cricketana can be viewed today by visitors to Lord's.

A number of letters to Rockley from other collectors or dealers survive. These reveal the extent of Rockley's interests in cricket books and history. For example, he enquired of J.W.Overend, proprietor of the Overend Press, in 1923 about the possibility of getting copies of two Overend publications, *Cricket for Boys* and the *Eccleshill C.C. Record Book.* Mr Overend replied that neither

---

35   Some details of the catalogue can be found in David Wilson, The Rockley Wilson Collection in *The Journal of the Cricket Society*, Autumn 1988, pp.51-54. Irving Rosenwater includes Rockley Wilson in his little book, *Cricket Books: Great Collectors of the Past*, privately published in 1976.

was in print but, as "I certainly do know your name and have seen you play on more than one occasion," he was pleased to loan Rockley a copy of the *Eccleshill Record Book*. Unfortunately copies of the letters sent by Rockley have not survived and we cannot know why he was interested in that particular club at that time. Of more curiosity interest among the correspondence is a letter dated 24 December, 1944 from Colonel Douglas Clifton Brown, then Speaker of the House of Commons and later Viscount Ruffside. In thanking Rockley for the gift of an unusual print of Speaker's House and St Stephen's Chapel, the Speaker comments that they had not met since their Trinity College days and asks "I wonder if you still play cricket" adding "I'm afraid I gave it up many years ago." But then few of Rockley Wilson's contemporaries could match the span of years over which he continued to play the game at a serious level.

Blessed with an exceptional memory, Rockley Wilson was a walking encyclopaedia of cricket facts and statistics, always ready to put his knowledge to others' use. In the Wilson papers there is a letter dated 15 June, 1941 from Raymond Robertson-Glasgow seeking Rockley's help with an article that Robertson-Glasgow was intending to write for *Men Only* on "On Making 0." Recalling an occasion when King Edward VII, then Prince of Wales, made nought when playing for I Zingari in a match at Sandringham, bowled by "a probably insane and intoxicated opponent," Robertson-Glasgow adds "but could you, if you have a moment, of your lore and store let me have some news of famous noughts in any class of cricket."[36] Sadly there is no record of Rockley's reply to the request. In a more serious vein, in August 1952, Douglas Jardine bombarded Rockley "as the infallible source" with questions to prepare himself for a debate at Lord's on the issue of covered wickets. In Wilson's company, "*Wisden* was a waste of space."[37]

Rockley Wilson was a stylish writer and the pity is that he wrote so little on the game. He wrote occasional articles for *The Cricketer*, the editor of which was his friend Plum Warner. These articles were invariably on historical or literary subjects, for example, his articles Early Cricket at Rugby in *The Cricketer Spring Annual*,

---

36   The match was I Zingari against the Gentlemen of Norfolk in 1866 and the Prince of Wales was persuaded to play for I Zingari "bedecked in the full IZ array." See R.L.Arrowsmith and B.J.W.Hill, *I Zingari: the Club, the Cricket, the Characters*, updated by A.S.R.Winlaw, JJG Publishing, 2006, p.16.
37   Peter Thomas, *Yorkshire Cricketers, 1839-1939*, Derek Hodgson Publisher, 1973, p.234.

1940; Some Notes on Love's Poem, *The Cricketer Annual*, 1940; Early Cricket Prints in *The Cricketer Spring Annual*, 1941 and Frederick Lillywhite and his "Guides" in *The Cricketer Annual*, 1943. All are erudite essays; the one on Love's Poem, for example, is a piece of historical detective work that pinpoints the date, 1744, of the match between Kent and an All-England XI about which James Love wrote his celebrated poem. These articles demonstrate Rockley Wilson's deep interest in the history and literature of the game of cricket and the meticulous nature of his research. Had the history of sport been an academic subject in his day, he would surely have been one of its leading authorities. By contrast, he seems never to have written on contemporary cricket matters, except as a cricketer-journalist on MCC's tour of Australia in 1920/21, about which more anon. (After his career was over, he also steadfastly rejected any suggestion that he should write his memoirs.) Rockley's scholarship often surfaced in letters to his friends: one to R.L.Arrowsmith is headed "September 7th. Birthday of George Hirst and an anniversary of Cynaxa." and another "October 28th. This should reach you on October 29th, birthday of Wilfred Rhodes and also anniversary of the murder of the generals in Xenopha."

Rockley Wilson's weightiest contributions to cricket literature are his chapters in the *Badminton Library* volume on cricket, published in 1920.[38] They reveal much of the man. In a long chapter on bowling, which Neville Cardus described as "E.R.Wilson's brainy masterpiece"[39], Rockley traces the historical development of bowling and provides astute advice for all types of bowler, reinforcing his points by perceptive references to leading bowlers of his time in the game. A.W.Pullin, writing as "Old Ebor" said of this chapter, "It is the best, most complete and most lucid treatise on the art and craft of bowling which the bibliography of cricket contains."[40] Cricket and bowling have much changed since the 1920s, but the Badminton chapter can still be read for enlightenment as well as for enjoyment. Rockley's chapter entitled "The Art of Training Young Cricketers" is a more general coaching manual, dated maybe with its public schools context, but still highly instructive and laced with wise aphorisms. The chapter on "The University Cricket Match", written with Hon R.H.Lyttelton, is

---

38   P.F.Warner (ed.), *Cricket*, The Badminton Library, Longmans Green, 1920.
39   Neville Cardus, *Days in the Sun*, Rupert Hart Davis, 1948, p.138.
40   Quoted in Irving Rosenwater, Rockley Wilson, *White Rose*, May 1998.

a detailed year-by-year account of the history of matches between Cambridge and Oxford. Yet there is no mention of Rockley Wilson, notwithstanding that he played in four University matches, was captain of Cambridge in 1902 and, as already mentioned, in 1901 turned in one of the outstanding all-round performances in the history of the fixture. The editor, Pelham Warner, interjected this comment into the account: "Mr E.R.Wilson refrains, with becoming modesty, from mentioning his own performance in the University match; but he was one of the best cricketers Cambridge has had. ... He was also a most able captain." One has only to read these chapters of the Badminton book to be aware of the depth of Rockley Wilson's knowledge of the game, its history and its lore to appreciate how much he could have contributed to cricket literature had he only had the inclination.

As well as cricket books and cricketana, Rockley Wilson also had an eye for fine furniture and was something of an authority on silver and silverware. The wife of Rockley's eldest brother Rex was a member of a distinguished family of silversmiths and Rex was involved for many years in the Cutlers' Company in Sheffield. These connections may have been the source of Rockley's interest in silver. Whatever the stimulus, over the years he acquired some beautiful silver pieces. In the early 1900s, Rockley also became interested in philately, and stamp collecting was to become a serious hobby, as it was with his brother Clem. He was especially interested in British line-engraved issues.

Throughout his life Rockley maintained a close relationship with his family, particularly his brother Clem and his wife Adel[41], and his unmarried sister Phyllis, the youngest of his siblings. He was very fond of Clem's son David, to whom he was godfather, paying occasional visits and corresponding with him on family and cricket matters.[42] Rockley himself never married. While at Cambridge, his girl friend was killed in a railway accident.[43] Rockley was devastated. Although he enjoyed female company, as far as is known there were no more romantic entanglements. Nor, however, is there anything to suggest his relationships with his

---

41   Adel, daughter of the first Baron Hamilton of Dalzell, was Clement's second wife. His first wife, Evelyn Rose, died in 1909. That she and Rockley had a Christian name in common must be coincidence.

42   He would write to David on the backs of any piece of old paper, even a contract note for the sale of some shares and part of a town plan. He was too disorganised a person to leave systematic files of his correspondence.

43   Jeremy Malies, *Great Characters from Cricket's Golden Age,* Robson Books, 2000, p.220.

many male companions were more than friendship. Several members of the cricket 'establishment' were among his friends with Plum Warner perhaps the warmest of these. Not surprisingly given his interests, he counted such distinguished cricket writers and historians as Harry Altham, Bob Arrowsmith, Jim Swanton, and Raymond Robertson-Glasgow among his network of friends and acquaintances. According to Swanton, it was Rockley Wilson's library and deep knowledge of the game that inspired Harry Altham to write articles on cricket history that appeared in *The Cricketer* and in 1926 were published as Altham's celebrated *History of Cricket*.[44] Rockley was a gregarious person and inimitable company. He loved good food and conversation. Plum Warner commented that to dine with him was "an unforgettable occasion." Apparently, his practice was to place his guests at table as if he were setting a field!

Rockley Wilson was very much a man of his time and of his class, though he was more at home in the company of professional cricketers, with whom he would happily share a game of cards during rain breaks or when on tour, than many amateurs of his generation. He had none of the innate snobbery of a Johnny Douglas or Douglas Jardine. It is just as well or Rockley would have had short shrift from his professional colleagues in the Yorkshire side. We will have cause later to say something about ructions between Yorkshire and Middlesex in the 1920s that were fermented by class-consciousness on both sides and in which Rockley found himself cast in a mediating role. Meanwhile, it is worth mentioning an incident recounted by Patsy Hendren to which Rockley Wilson was an innocent party as it illustrates the class divide between the amateur and professional in cricket in his day. On the 1920/21 Ashes tour in Australia, Harry Howell, the professional fast bowler, acted as "sub-postman" for the party. On the first morning he handed one letter addressed to E.R.Wilson with the remark "'Ere y'are." Douglas thought this did not show the appropriate respect and remonstrated with Howell. Howell explained that he was saving time giving Wilson's full name by saying "E.R." which, he suggested, may have sounded like "'Ere y'are" when said quickly. Hendren doesn't say whether Douglas accepted the explanation or whether he, Hendren, believed it. The implications are "yes" and "no"![45]

---

44 E.W.Swanton, *The Writer*, in Hubert Doggart (ed), *The Heart of Cricket: A Memoir of H.S.Altham,* Hutchinson, 1967, p.161.
45 E.H.Hendren, *Big Cricket*, Hodder and Stoughton, 1934, p.47.

One subject in which Rockley showed little interest in his adult life was politics, although there can be no doubt which side of the political divide he supported when the occasion arose. During the 1926 General Strike, he signed on as a "special" probably more out of a sense of loyalty to the Government than any wish to defeat the miners and their trade union supporters. Even such an event he could embellish with his characteristic humour. He was allotted the number eleven in the temporary force and he recounted that the police officer commented "Your right place, Mr Wilson, No.11."

In short, Rockley Wilson deserves to be remembered as more than an excellent cricketer; articulate and cultivated, he was indeed a singular man.

Chapter Five
Winchester

It is time to return to the chronology of Rockley Wilson's life and cricket career. On leaving Cambridge, Rockley obtained a teaching post at Winchester College which had the reputation of being the most intellectual of the public schools, but which also had a fine cricketing tradition, and he played no more first-class cricket in England until 1913. He had in fact indicated to Lord Hawke that he would be willing to play for Yorkshire in the 1903 season, but he had to rescind this when he was asked to take up his post at Winchester earlier than he had expected in order to replace E.H.Buckland, who had fallen ill, as the master in charge of cricket. H.D.G.Leveson Gower claimed that he had recommended Wilson to Buckland as his successor after seeing Rockley's debut innings for A.J.Webbe's XI at Cambridge. His commendation read: "He is not only good at books but as far as cricket is concerned there cannot be anyone better to teach the youth. He is a very good batsman and his length is impeccable; added to this, his knowledge of cricket is prodigious."[46] Whether Leveson Gower's recommendation did bring about the appointment, his description of Rockley's qualities was spot on.

Yorkshire enquired as to Wilson's availability in the school holidays for the 1904 season, though it is a moot point whether he could have commanded a place in the strong Yorkshire side of the time. Anyhow, as he explained, "I told Lord Hawke that, as I was only going to get a month's cricket, I would rather play three matches a week than two, so I spent the summer holidays in 1903-12 playing country house two day cricket."[47] Lord Hawke suggested that the real reason for his decision was "because he knew he could not get enough bowling, and he was so fond of it he would have liked to bowl both ends."[48]

---

46   Sir Henry Leveson Gower, *Off and On the Field*, Stanley Paul, 1953, p.35.
47   A.W.Pullin, *History of Yorkshire County Cricket, 1903-1923*, Chorley and Pickersgill, 1924, p.232.
48   Lord Hawke, *Recollections and Reminiscences*, Williams and Norgate, 1924, p.280.

Rockley Wilson remained on the permanent staff at Winchester College until 1939 and continued to help with teaching during the Second World War. His subjects were French and Greek. For its pupils, life at Winchester was Spartan and discipline strict, with sport in the afternoons no doubt a welcome relief from the routines of the classroom for most of the boys. Rockley was no disciplinarian. His classes were often uproarious and more or less out of control, leading one of his headmasters to observe, with ironic understatement: "It would be an exaggeration to pretend that all boys who left his division were completely bilingual."[49] Punctuality and careful marking of his pupils' work were not among his qualities. There is a story of him dashing down a hill on his bicycle, late for a class, and colliding with a boy who cried "Oh Christ!" to which Rockley is said to have replied "But strictly incognito, dear boy, strictly incognito."[50]

His lessons were punctuated with cricketing terms and phrases. He would ask a pupil to begin a translation with "We'll give Smith the new ball" and, if Smith lost his place, Rockley might observe "perhaps you are bowling rather wide." "Rain stops play" would be his response when taken short in a lesson, as often happened. He was not averse to a bit of play-acting. He was once persuaded by his pupils to dress up in Arab clothes and mimic a Moslem at prayer, much to the boys' merriment and to his discomfort when the Headmaster entered the room. Rockley was always willing to provide private tuition to his pupils. Whether the subject was French literature or Greek grammar, the tuition was likely to be lightened by conversation about cricket and the offer of real Turkish delight and

Rockley Wilson in the classroom.

other delicacies. A fellow teacher at the school, F.C.Mallett, recounted that he asked a pupil how he was getting on and received the reply: "I am not very good at French but I'm up to Mr Wilson and he calls me 'the Sutcliffe of the side' so I think I shall

---

49   Obituary in *The Wykehamist*, 15 October, 1957.
50   Like other Rockley Wilson stories, this cannot of course be readily corroborated.

get quite a good mark." It is not surprising that Rockley Wilson was a very popular teacher, if not a particularly effective one. One of his ex-pupils, Peter Newbolt, was to write: "I remember very little of what Rockley was supposed to be teaching, but have more happy memories of him than of any other don at Winchester – which is saying quite a lot." Szeming Sze, son of the Chinese Ambassador to the United Kingdom and a pupil at Winchester from 1921 to 1925, remembered Rockley Wilson as "one of my favourite teachers. Besides coaching me at cricket, he used to teach me French. I used to go to his home once a week at one time for coaching in French and I remember the kindness of his sister who used to bring me tea with a large slice of fruit cake."[51] No doubt Rockley had a better rapport with his pupils in one-to-one coaching sessions than he did in the class-room, or "divs" in Winchester College parlance.

Whatever may have been his scholastic contribution, Rockley Wilson made a substantial contribution to cricket at Winchester.[52] He was in charge of cricket at the school from his arrival in 1903 until 1929, assisted by a professional, among whom at various times were the Yorkshire players Walker Wainwright, younger brother of the better known Ted, and Schofield Haigh. He was helped, from shortly before the war in 1914, by fellow-teacher H.S.Altham, whose enthusiastic approach to coaching well complemented Rockley's more restrained methods. It has to be said that he inherited from E.H.Buckland excellent facilities including five practice nets, a most efficient system of coaching, and a highly organised programme of intra-school matches within which talented boys could improve their game.[53] Rockley Wilson built on this foundation, bringing to bear not only his great knowledge of the lore and techniques of the game, but an ability to impart his knowledge and experience to the boys without fuss or bluster. Rockley "gentles" his colts, said one of his colleagues. According to R.C.Robertson-Glasgow, "As a coach he can have had few equals. He not only knew the game, science and soul, and, to

---

51   The writer has drawn on the Wilson papers and material provided by Miss Suzanne Foster, Winchester College archivist, for these recollections of Rockley Wilson. Mr Sze's cricket knowledge was somewhat lacking however as he says that Rockley's googlies "caused havoc among the Australian batsmen" on the 1920/21 tour.

52   E.B.Noel, in his book *Winchester College Cricket*, Williams and Norgate, 1926, observed that from his appointment in 1903 until the time of writing, Rockley Wilson "has devoted his skill and knowledge of the game to Winchester."

53   See the description in W.J.Ford's essay on Public School Cricket in K.S.Ranjitsinhji, *The Jubilee Book of Cricket*, William Blackwood and Sons, 1897, pp.310-312.

the finest shade, what a young player could be induced to learn, but, like Alfred Shaw, he could pitch the ball pretty well where he liked. "And now I'll hit you on the toe," he once said, and he hit it. In the middle, he was almost certain death to the firm-footed hitter and the shuffling prodder."[54] Rockley's advice to young bowlers is succinctly put in an article on bowling in *The Cricketer Winter Annual*, 1921-22: "Don't neglect length. Length is the most important thing in bowling. Don't be led away by the snare of a big swerve or a big break. The most effective ball is a good length ball which turns a little and comes quick off the pitch. Study your field for your own bowling and bowl to your field: and above all, remember length, length, length." Rockley was here describing the attributes of his own bowling.

Douglas Jardine was a pupil at Winchester from 1914 to 1919.[55] He wrote later that "there has probably never been a stronger galaxy or combination of coaching talent functioning at one and the same time as Mr E.R.Wilson, Mr H.S.Altham and Schofield Haigh who were all at Winchester at the same time"[56] though, as we shall see, Wilson was serving in the Forces for most of the time that the young Douglas Jardine was at Winchester. Wilson was an outstanding bowling coach but he did not neglect to implant in his young charges the essentials of batsmanship. According to Rockley, a youngster's batting potential could be assessed from how well he played leg-side strokes, particularly the on-drive, but he believed that youngsters should first be taught to master off-side strokes. "The stroke of primitive man must have been to the on-side for you will always find that the natural tendency of the small boy is to pull everything. My theory is that a boy will never have any difficulty learning all the on-side strokes if he has once mastered those on the off-side, for they will come natural to him."[57] A frequently quoted remark attributed to Jardine was that Rockley Wilson emphasised the importance of getting behind the ball in the following way: "When I play back and miss the ball, I like to see it hit Wilson." Jardine was one of many persons with whom

---

54 R.C.Robertson-Glasgow, *More Cricket Prints*, T.Werner Laurie, 1948, p.33.
55 Jardine's biographer has provided a fascinating account of life at the school during these years (when wartime privations compounded the harshness of the school's regular regimes). See Christopher Douglas, *Douglas Jardine: a Spartan Cricketer*, Methuen (Paperback Edition), 2003, pp.6-10.
56 D.R.Jardine, *Cricket*, J.M.Dent (Second Edition), 1945, p.133.
57 Interview in *Cricket*, 6 July 1905, p. 242.

Batting technique being refined.
Rockley Wilson coaching in the nets at Winchester School.

Wilson regularly corresponded in the latter part of his life.[58] In a
letter of 3 June 1957, Jardine observed that had England's batsmen
followed Rockley Wilson's precept against the West Indies in the
First Test, "that would have solved 80% of their difficulties." We
can be sure that Douglas Jardine himself followed Wilson's advice
to the hilt for one thing that he never lacked was physical courage.
Wilson clearly saw other sides of Jardine's character, however.
When news of Jardine's appointment as captain of the MCC team
to tour Australia in 1932/33 was announced, Rockley's prescient

---

58   Earlier he had been a poor correspondent. His brother Clem once remarked
      that the only way of being sure of a reply was to send Rockley a pre-paid
      telegram, and added that Rockley had the best collection of unused reply
      forms in the country.

comment was: "I think we will win the Ashes, but we may lose a Dominion."

Rockley Wilson was in charge of cricket at Winchester for twenty years, ten before the First World War and ten after it. During that time, thirty nine of his pupils went on to play first-class cricket, including twenty Blues, sixteen at Oxford and four at Cambridge. Two of Rockley's pupils went on to play for England, Douglas Jardine, and A.J.Evans who played in a single Test against Australia in 1921, though a number of others might well have achieved that distinction if they had been able to find more time in which to play first-class cricket. Hubert Ashton, for example, a dashing batsman who played for an all-amateur (and victorious) England XI against the Australian tourists in 1921 and periodically for Essex between 1921 and 1939, might well have been capped by England if the demands of his business career had not absorbed most of his time.

Club Cricketer

Rockley did not neglect his own game while at Winchester. As Lord Hawke had been advised, he enjoyed regular country house and club cricket in the years up to the outbreak of the First World War. There were plenty of opportunities for men who had learned their cricket at the great public schools and who had the necessary social connections – and occupations which allowed plenty of leisure time – to continue to enjoy the game. Many were sufficiently talented that they could have made their way in the first-class game had they chosen to do so. Despite the inroads of the programme of first-class cricket, country house cricket was still an important feature of the cricket and social landscape in Edwardian England. The landed gentry and the nouveaux-riches were keen to host cricket weekends, even cricket weeks, at their country houses. The participating teams included the great touring cricket clubs such as I Zingari, Free Foresters and Incogniti, school-based clubs such as the Old Wykehamists, Uppingham Rovers, Eton Ramblers and Harrow Wanderers, Oxford and Cambridge college sides, and teams from the armed services.[59] Some of the leading cricketers of the day might be involved though matches were played in an informal manner, the informality

---

59   The Wilson papers include an invitation to Rockley to play against the Royal Artillery in 1913, advising "You will be housed and victualled in a respectable fashion."

sometimes bordering on the frivolous. The handsome surroundings, and the good company, the hospitality and the entertainment to look forward to when stumps were drawn, added to the pleasure.[60] As Rowland Bowen put it, "an amateur cricketer of merit could spend a happy August staying in one great house after another playing good class cricket all the time and well housed and fed and wined – paying no more than his travelling expenses and suitable tips for the staff."[61] As "an amateur cricketer of merit" plenty of invitations to country house cricket weekends came Rockley's way, enabling him not only to enjoy the cricket and hospitality, but also to widen his circle of influential

"The social side of country house cricket", rarely better illustrated.
Sadly the place and date are not known.
Rockley Wilson is third from the left in the front row.

---

60   In his artful essay on country house cricket in *Cricket,* the Country Life Library of Sport, 1903, H.D.G.Leveson Gower puts decidedly more emphasis on the social side of country house cricket: "a bevy of nice girls are needed to keep us civilised." There will be dances, songs and games and "boy and girl alike know they may never meet again, but they won't waste time meanwhile" (p.347). He does not favour champagne lunches but rather "some big pies, cold chickens, a fine sirloin of English beef and a round of brawn washed down by good ale and luscious shandy gaff." (p.348). If this was typical lunch-time fare one can be sure the afternoon's play would be rather leisurely.

61   *Cricket: A History of its Growth and Development throughout the World,* op.cit., p.143.

acquaintances both in and outside the game. Rockley was prepared to travel long distances by train or motor car to indulge his enthusiasm for the more social form of the game of cricket. Country house cricket appeared tailor-made for a man of Rockley Wilson's background and personality.

It was not necessary for a cricketer in Rockley Wilson's social circle to commit himself to one cricket club – it was rather different in the Midlands and the North where league cricket had taken root by the end of the nineteenth century – and there were many clubs that were happy to have use of Rockley Wilson's talents, even if not on an exclusive basis. Among the several clubs that Rockley Wilson appeared for while on the staff at Winchester were MCC, Old Wykehamists, Quidnuncs (a club for former members of Cambridge University Cricket Club), I Zingari, Free Foresters, Butterflies, Yorkshire Gentlemen, Northern Nomads and Hampshire Hogs. He became a member of MCC in 1904 and thereafter the club was to be an important part of his life. As already noted, he had first appeared for MCC in 1902 against Yorkshire at the Scarborough Festival[62], but rather surprisingly he did not appear very often for MCC subsequently. His intermittent appearances for MCC and Ground[63] in outmatches, mainly against public school sides (including, on a number of occasions, Winchester College), were in 1904, 1911, 1914, 1915 and, after the First World War, 1920, 1921 and 1923. It is likely that Wilson treated these fixtures more as a social occasion than as a competitive match. His contributions with the bat were invariably modest and when he did bowl he contented himself with two or three wickets before coming off. Of his other clubs, I Zingari was surely a Rockley favourite. The club had an attractive fixture list, including many country house games, and the club's mission – to promote the popularity of cricket far and wide – and its rather bizarre rules and customs, not to mention the striking club colours, would have appealed to him. Free Foresters, of which his brother Rowland Alwyn was an active member, was another all-amateur club that Rockley was pleased to play for before and after the First World War. As was the way with country house cricket and the travelling clubs, we find that Rockley Wilson played at various times both for and against I Zingari and Free Foresters,

---

62   Non-members can be selected to play for MCC; indeed, it is a way of qualifying as a 'playing member' of the Club.

63   Teams representing MCC and Ground included a mix of members and those employed as professional bowlers on the ground.

and probably other clubs with which he was associated, too. Wilson once described his batting in club cricket as "more unscrupulous than in first-class cricket", but when he put his mind to it he did make some good scores, even hundreds. For example, in 1904 he scored 114 for Free Foresters against Green Jackets at Winchester. Similarly while he often contented himself with two or three wickets before coming off, there were occasions when he ran through even strong club sides.

Fully blazered.
Northern Nomads side at Market Drayton, Shropshire,
with Rockley Wilson seated right, wearing his Yorkshire cap.

In term-time, Rockley played for the Winchester Dons XI, invariably strengthened by one or two boys from the school, and also for Winchester City. It is not easy to find records of Rockley's performances for these clubs, but the reminiscences of a fellow Winchester 'don' after Rockley's death suffice to show that his skills, particularly as a bowler, were well to the fore. He describes how in one match when Rockley was bowling and he was fielding, "a biggish man with a rather convex front came in. Rockley moved me about 20 yards to the onside of the screen. Presently the bait was cunningly offered, just short of a half volley outside the off stump. I don't think I had to move a yard as the ball came nicely into my hands. Soon after, number eight came in, an even more convex figure. Rockley signed to me to be ready and almost at once it came exactly as before: it would have been a crime to miss it."[64] Rockley also regularly appeared in the annual fixture in which the staff played against the school. In 1925 he not only played, he took all six school wickets that were to fall.

---

64   *Hampshire Chronicle*, 27 July, 1957.

Chapter Six
Return to First-Class Cricket

In the winter of 1911/12, Rockley Wilson took what were to prove his first steps on the road back into first-class cricket. He was invited to join an MCC party of amateur cricketers to tour Argentina under the captaincy of Lord Hawke. This was the first visit to the country by an English cricket team and the last of the ten overseas tours that the indefatigable Lord Hawke led during his long playing career. The British community around Buenos Aires was one of the largest outside the Empire and cricket had been played there since early in the nineteenth century. However, organised cricket, with fixtures between teams from the English clubs, schools and businesses in the country had been established in Argentina for only about fifteen years at the time of MCC's tour. The purpose of the tour was to increase interest in the game and encourage its further development. The tour was also a useful opportunity for Lord Hawke to look after his various business interests in the country. His Lordship described the tour as "entirely a holiday sort of country house trip."[65] Even so the MCC party was a fairly strong one and included five players who were at some time captains of county teams, one of whom was A.C.MacLaren. Unusually for the time, but reflecting the social side of the trip, five of the twelve tourists were accompanied by their wives. Rockley Wilson's inclusion, so many years after his withdrawal from first-class cricket, would have been very gratifying and the tour an exciting prospect. We can imagine him persuading his Headmaster at Winchester that the learning experience of a visit to South America would more than justify a short period of absence from his teaching post.

The tourists were warmly received wherever they played. Every effort was made by their hosts to provide comfortable accommodation and travel between matches for their visitors though the tourists found the heat very trying – "about a million in

---

65   Lord Hawke, op.cit., p.276.

Languor and style.
Spectators attending an MCC match in Argentina, 1912.

the shade" as one of the party put it, to emphasise the point[66] – and the facilities at the grounds sometimes a little rudimentary, with pig sties adjoining the boundary at one of them. Six of the nine games played were won, one lost and two drawn. Of the three first-class matches against the Republic of Argentina, designated "Test" matches by the hosts but barely of county standard, two were won and one lost. In these matches, which attracted crowds varying between a few hundred and over two thousand depending on the state of the game, Rockley Wilson was top of the bowling averages with 17 wickets at 10.76, his accuracy proving a potent weapon against inexperienced opponents. His best return was six for 36 in the second innings of the second of the "Test" matches. His bowling certainly impressed Lord Hawke. With the bat, Wilson averaged 25.80 from six innings in the first-class matches. In one of these, the first innings of the first match of the three, Wilson scored 67 not out, out of 186, batting at No.10 in a last wicket stand of 106 with C.E.Hatfeild. The reward for such a competent display of batting was Wilson's promotion to opener in all the remaining MCC innings in the "Tests", but he achieved very little.

---

66   Ibid., p.278

The batting average of 25.80 is rather misleading therefore. In other fixtures, Rockley scored a century in the match against South of Argentina and in the final match of the tour, against North Argentina on an awkward pitch, he took six for 66 and, in the second innings when he was virtually unplayable, taking eight for 10 despite an injured hand. Later Lord Hawke presented Wilson with the ball, "suitably mounted and inscribed." Overall, therefore, Rockley could be satisfied with his performance and pleased to have had the opportunity to extend his cricketing experience in another foreign country.

The MCC side which played Northern Argentina
at Rosario on 9 and 10 March, 1912.
Rockley Wilson is second from the left on the front row.

Playing again for Yorkshire

After his return from Argentina, Rockley Wilson was invited by one of his colleagues on the tour, A.J.L.Hill of Hampshire, to play for that county. According to Rockley, "I accepted as I did not think Yorkshire would mind." He had, of course, alerted Yorkshire of his intentions and when Lord Hawke realised that Yorkshire could be about to lose a potentially valuable player, "they very kindly asked me to play again and I did so. ... My real reason for wishing to play first-class cricket again was to see for myself the changes in the game caused by swerve and googlies."[67] If this sounds a trifle unlikely, it needs to be remembered that Rockley Wilson was a serious student of the game. More to the point perhaps, he must have been keen to establish if his obvious talent was enough for him to succeed in the first-class game before advancing years ruled that out. And he would have been flattered to be sought after by his native county.

Now 34, Wilson returned to the Yorkshire side in 1913 in the school summer vacation, playing in six successive Championship matches and one other first-class match. He took six for 89 off 35.2 overs in his first game against Warwickshire, when Hirst and Haigh were unable to bowl because of injury, and made a useful 31 in Yorkshire's first innings batting at No.8. In his fourth match, against Essex at Bradford, which Yorkshire won by an innings and 48 runs, Rockley turned in one of his most remarkable performances. Batting at No.9, he and Major Booth put on 126 for the eighth wicket, Rockley finishing with 104 not out, when the Yorkshire innings was declared closed at 512 for nine wickets. He spent only one hour and 50 minutes at the crease, hitting two sixes, a five and thirteen fours. It is doubtful if he would have played so venturesome an innings – one of his sixes was a skied hit over the wicketkeeper's head and over the boundary fence – had he not spent the preceding ten years playing club cricket: and, it has to be said, he was never again to bat with such abandon in a first-class match. This was to be Rockley Wilson's only century for Yorkshire: in all first-class matches he posted four hundreds. In neither of the following Championship matches did Wilson achieve anything of note.

Yorkshire were second in the Championship in 1913. As a result of his exceptional innings against Essex, Rockley finished second in the Yorkshire batting averages in Championship matches with 36.80 from eight innings, in three of which he was not out. In all matches his average was 32.00. As to bowling, Wilson took 14 wickets at 21.92 in the Championship and 18 at 19.66 in all matches for Yorkshire, finishing fifth in the Yorkshire bowling averages behind the professionals Alonzo Drake, Major Booth, George Hirst and Schofield Haigh, but above Wilfred Rhodes. Rockley's other first-class appearance in 1913 was for Yorkshire

---

67   Pullin, op. cit., p.232.

against an England XI at Harrogate in mid-August. Yorkshire just failed to complete a convincing victory by an innings but, in truth, the opposition was hardly of England calibre. Nevertheless, Rockley could be pleased with his four for 11 off ten overs in the England XI's first innings.

This was a gratifying comeback to the first-class game and Rockley could have expected to improve on his performances in the following season. But by the time that Rockley was free of his teaching duties at Winchester in 1914, Great Britain was on the brink of war with Germany. He played in the match against Lancashire at Old Trafford that started on 3 August, the day before war was declared, and in the following match against Warwickshire. He made no impact in either game. The remaining matches of the 1914 season were played in a surreal atmosphere, with British troops already leaving for the front, and Rockley Wilson played no part in them. His place in the Yorkshire side was given to Tommy Birtles, a batsman. When the season was finally brought to a hurried close, first-class cricket was put aside for four long years.

Chapter Seven
Great War Interlude

It is rather hard to imagine Rockley Wilson as a soldier but, soon after the outbreak of war in 1914, he followed the lead of so many of his contemporaries and joined up; by then he was 35 years old. He was commissioned into the Rifle Brigade which had links with the city of Winchester. One of his postings was to a bicycle unit on the Isle of Sheppey, though apparently, despite his years at Cambridge, riding a bicycle competently was always beyond him. Among his duties was the organisation of the shipment of troops to France in the course of which he accompanied detachments to their reserve positions behind the front lines. As the full extent of the horrors of trench warfare unfolded in 1915, culminating in the battles of the Somme and Passchendaele in 1916 and 1917, Rockley must have been thankful to have a home-based posting.[68] After this spell of staff work, the Army opted to make better use of his talents. He studied Turkish at the School of Oriental Studies in London and qualified as an Interpreter (First Class), an achievement of which he was justly proud. In due course, in February 1918, Rockley was posted to General Headquarters of the Egypt Expeditionary Force as Staff Lieutenant and Intelligence Officer, first and briefly in Cairo and then in Palestine to an army base camp some twelve miles from Jaffa.

Rockley wrote regular letters to his brother Clem during his time in Palestine.[69] These fascinating documents reveal how perceptive an observer he was of the world around him. His letters are also laced with comments on his army colleagues, some rather cutting, and on life in the military, some rather irreverent. These comments were strictly for private consumption.[70] Rockley also used his

---

68   During the War, the Rifle Brigade suffered a total of 11,575 fatalities, most of them on the Western Front. The Brigade won ten Victoria Crosses.

69   Originals of Rockley Wilson's letters to his brother Clem were donated by David Wilson to the National Army Museum and are archived there.

70   He may have been difficult for superior officers to deal with. One exasperated commanding officer is said to have remarked: "Rockley, you may be the best slow bowler in England, but you're the worst bloody subaltern I've ever had in my battalion."

Members of the Turkish Interpreters Course at the School of Oriental Studies, London, probably 1917.
Rockley Wilson, with moustache, is third from the left in the middle row.

correspondence to endeavour to keep in touch with the cricket scene and the doings of his many cricketing friends and acquaintances, and also to further his own cricketing knowledge. Any person with some cricketing connection that he comes across in Palestine gets a mention in Rockley's letters. Here is a typical example which illustrates Rockley's encyclopaedic knowledge of the game: "I met an old Colonel Delacombe, DSO. A.F.Delacombe, brother of W.B., left hand bowler played for Derbyshire? 1885." The record books reveal that William Barclay Delacombe did indeed play for Derbyshire, in ten first-class matches between 1894 and 1900 and that he was the county's Secretary from 1889 to 1907.

The officers enjoyed a relatively comfortable life style. Each had an army servant to do the washing, mending and other menial tasks. The food was generally good and drink plentiful. But not everything was rosy: irritants included the summer heat, frequent sandstorms, flies and other unpleasant insects, and occasional German bombing raids. As to Rockley's military duties in Jaffa, these were varied and could be demanding. His section's responsibilities included the translation and interpretation of captured material and documents, the drafting of official letters and the writing of intelligence reports, and "the general substitution of British for German influence in Palestine" through the encouragement of trade and economic development and the fostering of closer relations with the indigenous population. Rockley relished this aspect of the work and the opportunities it gave to visit historic and religious sites in the area, absorb something of Islamic culture and improve his Turkish. There is little doubt that Rockley could have been a most successful travel writer. His letters contain vivid descriptions of journeys from Jaffa to Jerusalem and of the sights of the Holy City, of a visit to the Dead Sea (in which he refused to bathe on account of the dirtiness of the water), of a journey up the Jordan Valley to Jericho and the Sea of Galilee, and later to Damascus. Rockley was deeply affected to be in places known to Jesus Christ and his Disciples. The flora and fauna of the region also interested him greatly. He has little to say however about the local people he would have encountered on his travels. As was typical of the officer class at the time, Rockley had a rather low opinion of the Arabs and their Turkish masters.

Rockley also took every opportunity during his time in the Middle East to acquire stamps for his collection. By the end of the war he had amassed a large number, some of which proved to be rare. He had an eye for antiques and objets d'art. Among his purchases were carpets, leatherware and fine silks which he thought would make "pretty frocks" for his sisters.

There are many anecdotes about Rockley Wilson's time with the army in Palestine. In one of the best an officer in the Australian Light Horse, boasting of his men's exploits, remarked: "Last week my men were encamped on the hills above Bethlehem", whereupon Rockley broke in "I bet the shepherds watched their flocks <u>that</u> night."

Cricket provided enjoyable interludes from military duties in the Middle East, as in other theatres of war, and Rockley played in various Army matches (but not, because of pressure of work, in the "Test" matches, so-called, between teams from Cairo and Alexandria). As would be expected, he had a considerable degree of success. In a letter to Clem, he remarked: "I can generally get a few wickets on the queer pitch where we play." This was a matting wicket. Rockley reports in another letter that one match had to be scrapped when it was discovered that Bedouin tribesman had stolen half of the matting! The outfields were sometimes coarse grass, but more often sand and stones. "A ground shot seldom counts more than one, however truly hit."

"Lt E.R.Wilson b Sgt Kelly 5"
in the match GHQ Officers v Sergeant
Majors and Sergeants is the formal story.
This picture of the match in Palestine in 1918
gives an idea of the conditions.

In October, 1918, Rockley attained the rank of Captain, though he said he did not "care a blow" about the promotion. By then it was clear that the end of the war was approaching. But after the Armistice was signed, Rockley's de-mobilisation was delayed by riots in Palestine and Syria over the failure of the Allies at the Peace Conference in Versailles to grant self-determination to the Arabs. He was posted to Aleppo, an Arab city in northern Syria and one of the oldest inhabited cities in the world – he said its citadel reminded him of Scarborough Castle – where he spent the early months of 1919 on economic and political intelligence work. It was not until May, 1919 that Rockley was able finally to leave the army and look forward to renewing his teaching career at Winchester.

Rockley Wilson therefore had an interesting and not especially dangerous war. Others were less fortunate. Yorkshire's Major Booth (Major was his Christian name, not a military rank) was killed at the Battle of the Somme in July, 1916, and Alonzo Drake, who had been in poor health before 1914, died shortly after the war. Although he could hardly have expected it during his sojourn in the Middle East, these tragedies, and the retirement of Schofield Haigh, who as already mentioned went to Winchester College as the professional coach, were to open the door for Rockley Wilson to stake a regular place in the Yorkshire side in the school vacations.[71]

Palestine General Headquarters Officers' Mess, 1918.
Standing (l to r): Lt Smith, Capt J.de V.Loder, Lt B.Sanders, Lt Clapham,
Lt Scott-Archer.
Seated: Capt E.W.Duffield, Maj G.le R.Burnham, Maj V.Vivian, Rev J.de la Bere.
On the ground: Cap O.C.Harris, Capt E.R.Wilson, Capt R.H.Cawston.

After the enforced interlude of the war years, Rockley Wilson was apparently so little remembered in Yorkshire that the *Yorkshire County Cricket Yearbook* of 1919, in its feature *List of Players Since 1833*, had his name as E.Rodley Wilson and his date of death as 13 August 1906, fifty one years before his time! The error was corrected, without comment, in the 1920 edition.

---

71   In one of his letters to Clem, Rockley noted the sad news of the death of Alonzo Drake and added, presciently, "[Yorkshire] will need a fresh set of bowlers to help Wilfred as I don't think George Hirst will bowl much more."

Chapter Eight
First-Class Cricket After the War

The First World War brought fundamental changes to British society. The trades unions and the Labour Party emerged much strengthened, and on both the industrial and the political fronts there was growing pressure for improvements in the conditions of working people. Women who had worked in their thousands during the War on farms, in factories and in hospitals were no longer willing to accept the subservient status they had generally had in Edwardian society. These developments, coupled with high taxation and inflation, bore heavily on the upper class. Men – less so women – without the benefit of wealth and property could aspire to leading positions in politics, industry and the professions. Britain was inching her way towards a more democratic and egalitarian society. But little changed in cricket. At Lord's, the officers and committees of MCC continued to be filled very largely by men of rank and privilege. There was no place for women. The position was similar in many county clubs. Oxford v Cambridge, Eton v Harrow and Marlborough v Winchester were still major fixtures in the cricket and social calendar. The ranks of the amateurs in first-class cricket were much reduced after the War, but most County elevens included at least some amateurs and all would have an amateur captain, indeed would do so with minor exceptions, until after the Second World War. The amateurs still typically travelled, dined and were accommodated separately from their professional team-mates. Indeed cricket was organised after the War much as it had been in Edwardian times.

Two-day cricket

There was one innovation for the 1919 season. The experiment was tried of limiting County Championship matches to two days instead of three and extending the hours of play on each day, taking advantage of the wartime daylight saving scheme. The hope was that the change would encourage people to go to grounds after work and so would lead to larger attendances. Rockley

Wilson was discouraged by the change. In February, 1919 he wrote to Clem from Palestine: "I am afraid I shall be too old to have another go with these hours, even if Archie White [the Yorkshire captain in the final season before the War] wants me." The Yorkshire club had not welcomed the new system either, but the team found it sufficient to their liking to win the Championship under a new captain, D.C.F.Burton, and with a team that – like many others – had to be rebuilt after the War.[72] Its success reflected the depth of talent available to the club. There had been some concern about the lack of good amateur cricketers capable of taking on the captaincy and some commentators bemoaned the fact that Rockley Wilson was only available for a short period each summer. David Burton had made his first-class debuts for Cambridge and for Yorkshire in 1907 but did not appear regularly for the county until 1914. However, after the War, he was to prove a useful batsman and an imaginative captain.

On his return from his military service, Yorkshire's need to supplement their bowling resources meant that, despite his own misgivings about the two-day format, the club did call on Rockley Wilson's services when he was available in the school summer vacation. By then he had played some club cricket and had turned out for Pelham Warner's XI against the Public Schools XI in a two-day match at Lord's. By taking three for 75 off 33.4 overs in the Public Schools' first innings and two for 62 off 26 overs in the second innings, he had perhaps convinced himself that he had the stamina to return to the first-class game: he would never have doubted that he had the skill.

In the month of August, Rockley appeared in eight successive two-day Championship matches between 8 August and 30 August, a hectic schedule of cricket and travelling even for a younger man than Rockley. In the first of these matches against Leicestershire at Leicester, which Yorkshire won by an innings and 126 runs, Rockley scored 51 runs and with Arthur Dolphin put on 62 runs for the ninth wicket. It was to be his highest score of the season and his last fifty for the county. Bowling was to be his forte hereon.

---

72   By another change this season, the championship was awarded to the team with the largest percentage of wins, not all teams playing the same number of matches at this time. It was not until some hours after Yorkshire had finished their final match and they heard that Kent had failed to beat Middlesex, that they knew they were champions. Kent had played only 14 matches, Yorkshire no fewer than 26, of which 12 were won. See Pullin, op.cit., p.148.

Rockley later felt that his break from serious cricket during the war years had a beneficial effect on his bowling. He did not know the reason, but after the War he was able to obtain a little more pace off the pitch, possibly because he brought his left foot down at the point of delivery rather more vigorously. For a slow bowler, Rockley certainly made unusually deep indentations in the pitch. Whatever the reason, in 1919 Wilson was third in the Yorkshire bowling averages behind the veteran Wilfred Rhodes and Roy Kilner, all of the leading three therefore being slow bowlers, though the emergence during the season of the fast-medium left-arm bowler Abram Waddington was gratifying for Yorkshire's future. Wilson's best bowling performances in the Championship were three for 58 and three for 56 (out of only four wickets to fall) against Surrey at The Oval, four for 35 against Middlesex at Headingley, and six for 28 off 18.3 overs on a perfect batting wicket and two for 64 in the second innings in the return match against Middlesex at Lord's. In the Championship, his batting average was 15.16 and he took 26 wickets at 16.03.

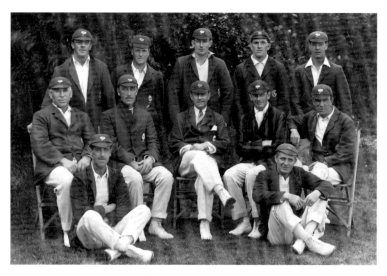

Return to normalcy.
The Yorkshire side which won the County Championship in 1919.
Standing (l to r): A.Dolphin, R.Kilner, A.Waddington, A.C.Williams, H.Sutcliffe.
Seated: G.H.Hirst, W.Rhodes, D.C.F.Burton (captain), E.R.Wilson, D.Denton.
On the ground: P.Holmes, E.Robinson.

Wilson played in three other first-class matches in 1919, all of them three-day affairs, two at the Scarborough Festival in September and one the annual Champion County match against the Rest of England at The Oval. Yorkshire lost the match against the Rest by ten wickets, Rockley bowling 40.5 overs in which he took three for 134, as the Rest piled up 493 with Jack Hobbs and Frank Woolley both scoring hundreds. In Yorkshire's match against MCC at Scarborough, Wilson returned his best bowling figures of the season, seven for 46 in MCC's first innings, a performance that may have resonated at Lord's more than did the results he achieved in the Championship, and he also figured in another valuable partnership with Arthur Dolphin when Yorkshire had been reduced to 123 for eight wickets, the pair putting on 47 runs. Selection for the Gentlemen against the Players fixture at the Festival seventeen years after his first appearance, when still at Cambridge, must have given Rockley a great deal of pleasure, though in the match the pleasure was alloyed with more toil. The Players won easily by an innings and 110 runs. In the Players' only innings of 397, in which Jack Hobbs and J.W.Hearne both scored centuries, Rockley Wilson took four wickets for 102 runs off 42 overs. This marathon bowling performance included the hat-trick with which Wilson finished off the Player's innings, his victims being George Hirst (bowled), Alec Kennedy (stumped) and Arthur Dolphin (bowled). It was the first time the feat had been achieved in the fixture at Scarborough.[73]

Photographs taken in 1919 show Rockley wearing a Yorkshire cap. It is not known when the cap was awarded as records were not kept at the time. Before the First World War Yorkshire caps were in the sole gift of Lord Hawke, even after he had relinquished the captaincy. Lord Hawke had had a high regard for Rockley Wilson's abilities from his Cambridge days and the two men were on good personal terms. It seems likely that his Lordship would have awarded Rockley his cap at some date before the War.[74] What is certain is that Rockley always wore his Yorkshire cap with pride, even sometimes when bowling.

In the early months of 1919 when Captain Rockley Wilson was engaged on intelligence work in inhospitable country in Syria, by

---

73   This feat is perhaps unrecognised. In Pelham Warner, *Gentlemen v Players, 1806-1949,* Harrap, 1950, the author's comments on the Scarborough match refer to Jack Hobbs' century, his third in the season in Gentlemen v Players matches, but makes no mention of Rockley Wilson's hat-trick.

74   This is also the view of Roy Wilkinson, the Yorkshire club statistician.

when he had passed his fortieth birthday, he could not have imagined that he would be able to look back at the end of the summer on so satisfactory a return to first-class cricket. His batting average in all matches was a modest 16.50, but it was as a bowler that he had impressed. In its review of the 1919 season, *Wisden* said of Rockley Wilson: "His slow bowling looks innocent enough, but he has great command over his pitch and there is something in the flight of the ball that makes batsmen expect a break that is not always there." In eleven first-class matches he took 40 wickets at an average of 17.47.

Three-day cricket resumed

The experiment with two-day games had proved unpopular, not least with the players, and was promptly abandoned. The 1920 season was a disappointing one for Yorkshire as they dropped to fourth in the Championship, arch-rivals Middlesex taking the title. But it was to be crowned with success for Rockley Wilson as it saw his selection in the MCC party to tour Australia for the 1920/21 Ashes series.

As in 1919 he played in only eight matches for Yorkshire in the Championship, and again these were all in the month of August. Norman Kilner was the player who usually had to give way to him. It was a punishing schedule, with one game followed immediately by the next. Of course, the game was less physically demanding in those days. One cannot imagine Yorkshire fielders of the 1920s throwing themselves around in the deep to save a boundary as is expected of modern players, Rockley Wilson perhaps least of all. And Rockley's easy and economical bowling action enabled him to bowl in long spells without taking too much out of himself. Nevertheless, the amount of bowling he got through was prodigious. In this 1920 season, he bowled 379.4 overs in the eight Championship matches, an average of more than 47 overs per match. These 379 overs, yielded Rockley 39 wickets at only 15.48 each. He finished second in the Yorkshire bowling averages.

In four of the eight matches Rockley Wilson took five or more wickets in an innings, an outstanding achievement in itself. In the first of these, a drawn match with Sussex at Headingley, he took five for 49 in Sussex's first innings. The next occasion was in the match against Middlesex at Bradford, when Rockley took three for 30 in the first innings and six for 62 in the second. Against Surrey at The Oval Rockley took four for 92 and five for 29, at one stage bowling for an hour without conceding a run, but could not prevent Surrey winning by 31 runs. In the final Championship match, Hampshire were beaten by an innings and 235 runs. Percy Holmes and Herbert Sutcliffe put on 347 for the first wicket, finishing with 302 and 131 respectively in Yorkshire's mammoth total of 585. Rockley Wilson then chipped in with five for 20 off 25.1 overs in Hampshire's first innings.

Rockley Wilson's value to the team did not rest just on the wickets he captured. His remarkable accuracy alone could be invaluable to his side – over the whole season he conceded only 1.59 runs per over. Neville Cardus had this to say about Wilson's bowling in the Roses match at Old Trafford: "Wilson, who bowled better than anybody else, got no wicket. ... Wilson is slow to medium and as fine a length bowler as we have in the game today. ... Wilson was always turning the ball. He varied his flight craftily, dropping a foot shorter without altering the upward trajectory. After lunch, in one spell of work, he sent down eight overs for three runs only."[75] Here the master of cricket prose acknowledges a master of the art of slow bowling.

As to his batting, Rockley averaged only 8.87 in the eight Championship matches and it was becoming very clear by this season that large scores could no longer be expected from him. However, he did figure in some useful stands in the lower order. In a low scoring and fluctuating match against Middlesex, Yorkshire required 198 to win on the final day but slumped to 140 for 8, with Roy Kilner ill and unable to bat. Rockley Wilson and Abram Waddington took the score to within four runs of victory when Waddington was bowled – by G.T.S Stevens, a nineteen year old Oxford University student, an indignity Waddington was never to forget – leaving Wilson 39 not out, his highest score of the season. Another last-ditch stand led to some controversy – it was not to be the last such occasion. In the match against Leicestershire on the August Bank Holiday weekend, a rain-curtailed match was destined to be decided on a one innings basis. It was important to Yorkshire's remaining hopes of winning the Championship that they were not dismissed for less than the Leicestershire score in their one innings. As the Championship points system ignored matches where no first innings decision had been reached, a "no

---

75   Neville Cardus, *The Roses Matches, 1919-1939*, Souvenir Press, 1982, p.54.

result" was a better outcome than a drawn match with points awarded for first innings. Only two runs were needed by Yorkshire with their last pair of Dolphin and Wilson at the wicket but the lead eluded them, the match thereby ending as "no result". Whether or not the criticism that the batsmen did not try to go for the runs is justified, it is significant that when Leicestershire sought agreement to play an extra half hour in an effort to get a result one way or the other, the Yorkshire captain, D.C.F.Burton, would not consider it.[76]

Wilson played in four other first-class matches in 1920 after the close of the championship season. By then he had been selected for MCC's tour of Australia. Taking these matches into account, Rockley finished the season with a batting average of 13.44 and 64 wickets at a cost of 13.84. The four matches were for the Rest of England against Middlesex; the County Champions, at The Oval; for Yorkshire against MCC; for the Gentlemen against the Players; and for the MCC Australian Touring Team against C.I.Thornton's XI, all at the Scarborough Cricket Festival. The Rest of England side against Middlesex consisted largely of players who would shortly be leaving for Australia. The match was drawn, the Rest scoring 603 in their first innings with Jack Hobbs emphasising his pre-eminence among English batsmen with a double century. Rockley Wilson was the most successful of the Rest's bowlers taking four for 44 in Middlesex's only completed innings. In Yorkshire's match against MCC, captained, as was the Rest of England side in its match, by H.D.G.Leveson Gower, Rockley Wilson captured ten MCC wickets, four in the first innings and six for 29 off 15.4 overs in the second, in an easy Yorkshire victory by nine wickets. Wilson also had a good match for the Gentlemen, also captained by Douglas, taking three wickets in each of the Players' innings and batting out time in very poor light with David Burton, his Yorkshire captain, to secure a draw for the Gentlemen in a match in which they were decidedly second best. In the MCC Australian Touring Team match against C.I.Thornton's XI, which also included some of the tour party, the MCC team won easily by an innings and five runs, Wilson taking two for 17 in the opposition's first innings and two for 7 in one over in the second.

Scarborough was always among Rockley's favourite cricketing venues. He had played there several times over the years for club

---

76   This account is based on Pullin, op.cit., p.164.

sides. Notable among these were Northern Nomads for whom he turned in some excellent performances. In the early 1900s, when Clem Wilson was often also in the Nomads team, Rockley had several hauls of five wickets or more in a Scarborough innings, the best being nine for 23 in Scarborough's second innings and fifteen wickets in the match in 1905. These fixtures were part of the Scarborough Local Cricket Week. As we have seen, Rockley had first experienced the Scarborough Cricket Festival at the first-class level in 1902. In the 1920s, the Festival with its holiday atmosphere and large, good-natured crowds attracted by the participation of some of cricket's big names, was still a special occasion in the cricket calendar and one that appealed strongly to Rockley Wilson. Now among the best-known and liked of England's amateur cricketers and with a wide circle of friends in the game and in "society", Rockley could enjoy not only the cricket but also the socialising, dinners and entertainments that were the accompaniments to the matches. After this traditional end to the 1920 domestic season, Rockley would have been full of anticipation as he returned to Winchester for a few weeks before the start of the tour of Australia.

Chapter Nine
Australia and After

It may have been the highlight of his career, but Rockley Wilson was a surprise selection for the MCC tour of Australia in 1920/21.[77] He was not included in the party that was announced on 26 July, 1920 with R.H.Spooner as captain, a "happy choice" as *The Times* put it. By that date Rockley had yet to appear that summer for Yorkshire. But Spooner had played little cricket that season and was troubled by injuries: he had been badly wounded twice in the First World War. After some heart-searching, Spooner announced on 16 August that he would not be able to tour. The vice-captain, J.W.H.T.Douglas, was then invited to take on the captaincy, and the selectors announced that another amateur would be added to the party later, with P.G.H.Fender now being the only one, other than Douglas himself. On 18 August, by when Rockley Wilson had appeared in four games for Yorkshire in which he collected 17 wickets – and, as we have seen, impressed Neville Cardus – came the announcement that he was the chosen amateur. *The Times* described Wilson, somewhat unenthusiastically, as "a fine all-round cricketer, a good batsman and a very accurate bowler." There were some who applauded his selection however. E.H.D.Sewell, for example, thought not only that Rockley Wilson was the ideal man to go but also that he should have been captain of the side. Sewell thought the line "caught Hendren bowled Wilson" would be "one to keep the compositors busy before long." When Rockley approached his Headmaster at Winchester for leave of absence to enable him to accept the invitation, the response was a discouraging, "Who are the MCC and what are they doing in Australia?" Nevertheless, leave was granted. Later still, the selectors invited the all-rounder V.W.C.Jupp, who had turned amateur the previous season, to join the party but he declined and the additional place went to J.W.Hitch, the Surrey professional and quick bowler. The selectors may have had Jupp in mind to take

---

77   Much of the material in this chapter on the 1920/21 tour of Australia has previously been published by the writer in his article, Rockley Wilson's Only Test, *Journal of the Cricket Society*, Autumn 2005.

Douglas' place as vice captain. In the event, they handed that honour to Rockley Wilson. Percy Fender might have seemed the more logical choice as he had had a very successful first season as Surrey's captain, but Fender was never a favoured son of the cricket establishment, and was not much admired by his captain, Johnny Douglas.[78]

MCC party and supporters setting off in the rain from Tilbury to Australia, aboard S.S.Osterley in September, 1920.
The picture includes from left to right: E.H.Hendren, F.E.Woolley, A.Dolphin, H.Howell, A.Waddington, W.Rhodes, J.W.H.T.Douglas, P.F.Warner, E.R.Wilson, J.W.Hearne, P.G.H.Fender, J.W.H.Makepeace, F.C.Toone.

The consequence of all this was that if Douglas had fallen under a bus, or over the side of *S.S.Osterley* on the long voyage to Australia, then Rockley Wilson would have found himself the captain of England, and of a party which included such giants of the game as Wilfred Rhodes, Jack Hobbs, Frank Woolley and J.W.Hearne, as well as two other Yorkshire colleagues, Abram Waddington and Arthur Dolphin, the reserve wicket keeper. In the event, of course, no such calamity befell Douglas, and Wilson captained the side only in three up-country matches of little significance from a cricket point of view, even if important to the host communities. His greatest contribution as vice-captain was to relieve Douglas of some of the

---

78   As recounted in Richard Streeton, *P.G.H.Fender: a Biography*, Faber and Faber, 1981, p.97. Streeton commented that the two men were "poles apart in manner and outlook."

burden of speech-making at the many civic and cricketing receptions and functions with which the English cricketers were regaled on their long tour of the country. Rockley used his knowledge of the history and personalities of the game, and his natural quick wit, to good effect in his speeches. In Melbourne, on the eve of a match against Victoria in November, for example, "he kept all amused for a few minutes while he dived back into cricket history and brought out an anecdote or a set of figures for each of the past masters of the game that he spotted amongst the gathering."[79] It seems likely that his reputation as a speaker came to exceed his reputation as a cricketer on this tour.

The MCC side which toured Australia in 1920/21, losing all five Test matches.
Standing (l to r): A.Dolphin, J.W.Hitch, C.H.Parkin, F.C.Toone (manager),
F.E.Woolley, C.A.G.Russell, A.Waddington.
Seated: H.Strudwick, W.Rhodes, E.R.Wilson, J.W.H.T.Douglas (captain),
P.G.H.Fender, J.B.Hobbs.
On the ground: H.Howell, E.H.Hendren, J.W.Hearne, J.W.H.Makepeace.

England were beaten by Australia in all five Test Matches, the first such humiliation, and, not surprisingly, Douglas did not escape criticism of his captaincy. One of the criticisms was of his handling of his bowlers, and in particular his reluctance to give more opportunities to his slow bowlers who included Wilson and Fender. *The Observer*, for example, in its review of the tour in its

---

79   P.G.H Fender, *Defending the Ashes*, Chapman and Hall, 1921, p.32.

issue of 6 March, 1921, said that the most serious mistake committed on the tour was the omission of Fender and Wilson in all five Tests, adding magisterially that A.C.MacLaren and P.F.Warner would surely have included both in all five matches and thereby "materially improved the team's chances of victory": a rather fanciful speculation, it has to be said, given the strength of the opposition. But even before the series began, an Australian newspaper article was reflecting that Wilson's style of slow, accurate bowling could be very successful against young Australian batsmen who would be tempted "to have a go at him."

Rockley Wilson himself did not have a good opinion of Douglas. In a letter to his sister Phyllis after only two of the Test matches, he said that the captain was not a success because of "his disregard on the field of advice from the real experts" and his "peculiar gift for ruffling the feathers of the professionals – coming the colonel over them, as I have overheard it described." But Rockley reserved his strongest criticism for the disruption caused, he said, by the presence since the beginning of the tour of Mrs Douglas and her daughter-in-law. "It is very hard to like the man," he concluded. Rockley kept his strong feelings about his captain to himself and it seems that his views were not shared by all his team-mates. Cecil Parkin, for example, went out of his way in his various books to say how much he admired Johnny Douglas and to praise his captaincy. But it is likely that Rockley was piqued by a growing realisation that he was likely to play only a minor role on the tour, despite being the official vice-captain. It is also likely that Wilson's views on the effect of the presence of accompanying females were shared since, after the tour, MCC ruled that wives would not be allowed to accompany their player-husbands on future tours.

While Fender played in the last three Tests, Rockley Wilson's only appearance was in the Fifth and final Test at Sydney, when he may have got his chance as much because the two fast bowlers, Hitch and Howell, were unfit as for his own bowling abilities. At 42, he was the oldest cricketer to get his first cap for England except for James Southerton, who was 49 years when he played in the very first Test match in 1877.[80] Australia won the match by eight wickets, but Wilson emerged with some credit. He bowled excellently to take two for 28 in the first innings from 14.3 six-ball

---

80   Rockley Wilson might well have observed that, had there been earlier Test matches, Southerton would no doubt have been younger when he was first capped!

overs, bothering Gregory, in particular, in his innings of 93 with his restricting accuracy and one wicket for 8 in six overs in the second innings. Fender had five wickets but was much less economical. In England's two innings, Rockley totalled a modest 10 runs, but in the course of his first visit to the wicket he was subjected to much hostile barracking. This was not the first such incident on the tour and, as Rockley Wilson was a central figure in what became something of a *cause célèbre*, we need to say something here about it.

England players, including Rockley Wilson with umbrella,
visiting the Melbourne Cricket Ground,
shortly before the Fourth Test in February, 1921.

The barracking controversy

The first reported incident was in the third match of the tour against Victoria in Melbourne. England piled up 418 runs for three wickets declared in response to Victoria's first innings total of 274 and they then dismissed the State side for 85 on a nasty, rain affected pitch, Rhodes taking six for 39 and Woolley four for 27. It was the slow scoring of Jack Hobbs and J.W.Hearne in their innings of 131 and 87 respectively that raised the ire of some spectators. However, the barracking, which included such shouts to Hobbs as "What do you think the boundary is for?" was hardly venomous. (Hobbs scored only four fours in his innings, though it needs to be added that the bowlers concentrated on bowling outside the off stump to a packed off-side field.) Indeed, Douglas described it to the Press as "good natured and humorous", so there was hardly the making of a serious incident here.

It was at the country match against a Bendigo XV that the beginnings of more serious trouble blew up. Its real cause was the content of some of the reports that Rockley Wilson and Percy Fender had been commissioned to provide to certain British newspapers during the tour. It needs to be remembered that any amateur who toured Australia at this time would be out of pocket. Travel and accommodation costs would be met, but most other expenses fell to the player and these could add up to a tidy sum. It is not surprising that the erudite Wilson jumped at the chance to earn some money as a part-time journalist. After *The Times* had published a piece about the outward sea journey, he was invited to write regular articles for the *Daily Express*: Percy Fender wrote for the *Daily News*. Rockley's reports on the first matches of the tour were wholly factual accounts of the cricket. He then received a cable from his editor: "Reuters report play adequately. We want comment." Rockley endeavoured to oblige. During the First Test at Sydney that preceded the game at Bendigo, he had cabled a report that included some criticism of the umpiring – the umpires in those days being provided by the host country, of course. According to Wilson, Waddington's run out in England's first innings was "a shameful decision" and he added that both Woolley and Douglas were the victims of "doubtful decisions" in England's second innings. Umpire A.C.Jones protested to the Australian Board of Control and Wilson was forced to apologise for the severity of his comments on the Waddington decision. But he added, after the match, "I still consider that Waddington was not out." These criticisms were widely reported in the Australian papers, national and local. The player-cum-journalists found that their cabled reports intended for British readers were soon relayed back to Australia, and part of the crowd at Bendigo consequently gave Wilson the bird when he came to the crease, branding him a "bad sport." Characteristically, he responded by bowing to the crowd. Douglas and Wilson complained about the barracking, however, and suggested that the authorities should take steps to stop it. This led the mayor of the township to say that Wilson's sarcastic reaction to the crowd's shouts made him the responsible party. It was reported that Wilson responded that he would see that MCC never visited Bendigo again, though Rockley strongly denied he had said any such thing. After this match, Rockley wrote to his sister that he was the most unpopular man in Australia. Did he but know it, his popularity was destined to sink even lower.

Travelling immediately after the Second Test at Melbourne by train to another country match against a Ballarat XV, a game where Rockley captained the MCC side, he was involved in a bizarre incident that led to more criticism and unpleasantness. He was playing cards with his overcoat over the players' knees for a table when the coat, with some valuables in the pockets, was suddenly whisked through the carriage window. The communication cord was pulled and the items quickly and successfully recovered, but Rockley was reported for pulling the communication cord without justification and inconveniencing other passengers. There is some dispute whether or not it was Rockley who stopped the train, but it was certainly Rockley who was pilloried when the story was reported in the newspapers as "the man who stopped our train." One irate Australian even sent him a miniature lavatory chain with his abusive letter: the letter remains among the Wilson papers – but not the chain.

After these incidents, Wilson was regularly barracked by the Australian crowds at any match and, in his turn, so was Fender. It got to such a pitch that police protection was requested for the MCC team for the second match against Victoria in February that was immediately to precede the Fourth Test at Melbourne. The request, which hardly endeared the tourists to the crowd, was refused. In the Test, Fender was noisily barracked, a section of the crowd shouting in unison **P**lease **G**o **H**ome Fender, a chant that was taken up on all his subsequent appearances on the tour.

It was in the final Test at Sydney, however, that the most serious incidents occurred. It all began when England took the field in the final stages of the first day, having scored only 204 in their first innings. Jack Hobbs had torn a thigh muscle in the previous match against New South Wales and had only agreed at the last minute to play in the Test, and then only under a deal of pressure from his captain. Hobbs was much handicapped in the field and his laboured running after the ball was greeted with derisory shouts from the crowd. Although most of the crowd were unaware of Hobbs' injury, Wilson and Fender chose to criticise the behaviour of the crowd in their reports to their newspapers. To a modern eye, the reports hardly seem explosive. For example, Wilson wrote "It was unworthy of a Sydney crowd to jeer at Hobbs running lame as a certain section did." On the second day, by when the crowd were aware of the criticisms made of them, Wilson had to join Rhodes at the crease when England had stumbled to 14 for two in their second innings and he was roundly booed all the way to the crease. When play was resumed after the Sunday rest day, and Rhodes was out, Hobbs was warmly applauded as he walked to the wicket, the crowd, now obviously having learned of his handicap when fielding, even chorusing "For He's a Jolly Good Fellow." In contrast, Wilson was again loudly barracked during his innings and when he returned to the pavilion on his own dismissal, having added but a single to his overnight four, some in the crowd chanting the letters L I A R, others shouting "Squealer" and "Go home" and still others just booing and jeering "like animals" as Cecil Parkin put it. Upset by the reaction, Wilson remonstrated with the crowd until shepherded into the pavilion by Harry Makepeace and M.A.Noble, the intervention of the veteran Australian cricketer quickly quelling the barracking, at least that from the members. Noble also persuaded the members to receive Fender in complete silence when he emerged to bat, advice that was largely followed if only by spectators in the pavilion. When England again took to the field, Wilson's weak throwing also encouraged a volley of uncomplimentary shouts such as "Throw it up, Miss Wilson." Similar rounds of booing and name-calling greeted Wilson in his final appearances of the tour.

These incidents at Sydney sparked a spate of comment in the Australian newspapers, with several correspondents attempting to explain the barracking away as the work of a few on the Hill, worse for wear for drink. Others criticised Wilson and Fender for failing to say in their cables that the behaviour of the great majority in the crowd had been sympathetic to Hobbs, the line taken by the leader writers. Fender responded with a letter to the *Sydney Morning Herald* in which he said he had reported what he had heard on the field of play and was surprised the Press had not "given a taste of the lash" to those spectators who had been unable to control their language or discriminate between "harmless fun" and "other things." Confronted by reporters at the end of the third day's play, Wilson said the papers had quoted selectively from his cabled report on the first day's play, and that he was astonished at the conduct of the barrackers, particularly those who had abused him in the members' stand, and added "such treatment as was accorded me today might have been expected in any country except Australia. I do not care what people who are capable of such things think of me. You saw how the crowd behaved: is that not a better answer than anything I can give you?" Fender and Wilson had hardly gone out of their way to cool the resentment against them.

It is worth pausing to reflect on what might have provoked the angry behaviour of certain of the spectators. No doubt Australian crowds were always more inclined to give vocal expression to their feelings about the play and the players than were their English counterparts (Bramall Lane notwithstanding) and it should be added that they were not averse to giving their own players the bird, at least in domestic matches. No less a player than Warwick Armstrong himself was frequently the butt of ribald comments from the crowd, and E.R.Mayne, the captain of Victoria, went so far as to suggest that barracking could destroy the confidence and careers of young players. Even when directed at the tourists, the barracking would usually be good-natured however, as it had been at Melbourne in the first match with Victoria mentioned above. Most Australians still had warm feelings towards the "Mother Country" bonded by the shared experiences of the First World War. However, in the early 1920s the Australian economy was depressed, unemployment high, and living standards generally low. There was some resentment that, after the sacrifices of Australia's young men, particularly at Gallipoli, Britain was not doing enough to help Australia to get back on her feet. Australian crowds, some with memories of the British officer class during the War, could easily be aroused by any perceived insults from English amateur and upper-class cricketers such as Douglas, Fender and Wilson (and later, of course, Jardine) or by any of their shortcomings on or off the field. It needs to be added that the Test series had been very keenly anticipated in Australia with immense media interest. The overwhelming success of Warwick Armstrong's team gave the keyed-up crowds plenty to cheer about and many opportunities to turn the knife in the England team's failings, sometimes in what must have seemed a hurtful way. It was the personal nature of the barracking rather than the barracking as such which deeply offended Rockley Wilson.[81]

Naturally, the British Press was inclined to blame the Australian crowd, sometimes rather patronisingly. The *Daily Express*, which had hired Rockley Wilson, observed in a leading article on 1 March, 1921 that "the whole thing is wretched" and went on to say: "If Tests are to continue at all, if cricket is to keep its place as a clean and wholesome game, the decencies of sportsmanship must be preserved all over the ground, not only inside the boundaries." *The Observer*, on 6 March, 1921, said "barracking of any sort is, and will ever be, offensive, always repugnant, never sporting, always provocative of retaliation, and certainly shocking and bad manners since no well-bred person ever has, or ever would, barrack" – a high-minded opinion indeed, though one Rockley Wilson would no doubt have shared. On 2 March, *The Times* came closer to the heart of the matter. It criticised the barracking and the "occasional heated questioning of umpires' decisions" as "entirely foreign to the spirit of the game" but added that the problem was exacerbated "by the tone of certain journalistic messages sent home by members of the English side." It considered the practice of cricketers on tour writing about the games "undesirable and harmful" and concluded that no one should be selected to play for his country without the understanding that "when he becomes a Test player, he lays down his pen."[82]

---

81 One England player who took a generous view of the barracking was Cecil Parkin. He liked the Australian crowds, admired their enthusiasm for the game, and thought that the barracking added to the interest and entertainment of the proceedings: see Cecil Parkin, *Cricket Triumphs and Troubles*, Nicholls and Co, 1936, p.70. But by background and personality, Parkin was more likely to empathise with an Australian crowd than were most of his team-mates.

82 This account of the barracking incidents is drawn largely from newspaper reports of the time, but also Streeton, op.cit., Malies, op.cit., E.H.Hendren, op.cit., and Jack Hobbs, *My Life Story*, The Star Publications, 1935. It has to be pointed out that Jeremy Malies' account of the barracking at Sydney Cricket Ground is incorrectly said to have been at the MCC v New South Wales match, the match in which Hobbs incurred his injury, not the Fifth Test match in which barracking of Hobbs' laboured fielding sparked the incident. A great curiosity is that Fender's book, *Defending the Ashes*, op.cit., written in the immediate aftermath of the tour, has virtually no comment on the barracking or its cause. A reviewer in *The Cricketer*, 23 July, 1921, commented: "Without Mr Fender's views on controversial matters, the book has the appearance of a censored letter home from the front, when Tommie wants to tell the home-folk what he thought of plum and apple and the shell shortage."

Aftermath

While a present-day reader would not find the reports of Rockley
Wilson and Percy Fender particularly controversial or one-sided –
Wilson had roundly criticised the "sloppy fielding" of the England
side in the First Test, for example – in the context of the time the
strictures of *The Times* are understandable. MCC certainly thought
some action was needed and so Wilson, Fender and the captain,
J.W.H.T. Douglas, were in due course called to Lord's to be
interviewed by the President and Treasurer. Although the
President reported that the "explanations given by these cricketers
was satisfactory," a critical motion was put down in the name of Sir
Charles Bright[83] for discussion at the Annual General Meeting
arranged for 4 May, 1921. It read "That the reporting for the Press
on matches by those who take part in them is not in the best
interests of Cricket, and that all possible steps should be taken to
discourage the practice." According to *Wisden*, the motion was
carried, but it appears that the MCC Committee pre-empted any
debate on the matter by referring it to the Board of Control for Test
Matches. The Board took the firm line advocated by *The Times*. Its
minutes of 19 April, 1921 record: "The Board of Control accepted a
suggestion from the MCC Committee, and have advised the
Selection Committee that when inviting anyone to play for
England, it shall be on the condition that the player does not
contribute a report or a statement of any kind to the Press, until
the end of the season, as regards any Test Match for which he is
selected and in which he plays."[84] Tour contracts since then have
endeavoured to control the practice: for example, the Conditions
of Employment of today's contracted England players include
detailed rules governing any public statements, and any written or
broadcast comments, on matches or on matters of "general cricket
interest."

As it was MCC policy that required the captain to be an amateur
and other amateurs to be included in the touring party, it could be
argued that it was incumbent upon MCC to recognise the financial
difficulties faced by some touring amateur players, perhaps by
permitting more generous payment of their expenses. For a player

83 Sir Charles Bright (1863-1937), whether by coincidence or not, an authority on
    submarine telegraphy, played minor matches for MCC and was an enthusiastic
    supporter of Essex.
84 There is apparently no reference to the Sir Charles Bright motion in the
    minutes of the A.G.M. The writer is grateful to Ms Glenys Williams, MCC
    Archivist and Historian, for this and other information on MCC's actions.

JOHNNY DOUGLAS (to Fender and Wilson) :
" There you are. You will play with printers' ink, instead of
playing cricket. You'll never wash that off."

Cartoon from a Sydney newspaper depicting, with perhaps a little sympathy, the plight of Wilson and Fender following their cables to English newspapers.

as educated as Rockley Wilson, journalism was an obvious source of earnings while on tour. His aim was to write interesting, well-informed accounts for the cricket-loving public in England. He would have denied that it was any part of his purpose to stir up controversy, but he may not have understood the workings of the mass-circulation newspapers. Perhaps he should have borne in mind the risk to which Jack Hobbs drew attention in his own comment on the incidents to which he was witness. "One moral from the whole affair is the lesson it teaches to those responsible for handling the news cabled from one country to another. By emphasising extracts in as sensational way, they give a distorted view of the facts and damage the relations between the two nations."[85] A safe conclusion is that the business did the Test careers of Rockley Wilson and Percy Fender no good at all.

In fact Rockley Wilson was never again selected to play for his country. The Australians were the visitors in the 1921 domestic season, with the Australian party and Douglas' defeated MCC party travelling to Britain on the same ship. Warwick Armstrong's side carried on where they had left off in Australia, winning the first three Tests to make it eight victories in succession against England. Wilson would have been available for the Fourth Test at Old Trafford which immediately followed Yorkshire's match with the Australians at Bramall Lane in which Rockley Wilson did play. Throughout the summer the selectors had been ringing the changes in the side, including replacing Douglas as captain by the Hon L.H.Tennyson after the First Test. Wilson was not selected for the Fourth Test however, or for the final Test at The Oval, both of which were drawn to provide some modest consolation for the home side. It is not particularly surprising that the selectors did not turn to Rockley at this late stage in the series, however good were his performances in county cricket. The England teams had been shown to be inadequate in batting (with Jack Hobbs' absence throughout from injury and illness being a grievous loss), quick bowling and fielding. England's fielding in the Second Test prompted *Wisden's* editor to observe, "Never before was an England side so slow and slovenly." It is hard to see how, at the age of 43 years, Rockley Wilson could be expected to make good any of these deficiencies. And as to later Tests, there was no overseas tour in 1921/22 and no Test matches in the domestic 1922 season. By the time that an MCC team needed to be chosen for the 1922/23 tour of South Africa, under the captaincy of F.T.Mann, Rockley Wilson's first-class career, let alone his Test career, was clearly drawing to a close. So Rockley Wilson became a member of the "one Test club." We can guess that Rockley would have taken wry satisfaction from the knowledge that he was joining a company of many other well-known cricketers.

---

85   Hobbs, op.cit., p.186.

Chapter Ten
Back to County Cricket

The tour of Australia had been a chastening experience for Rockley Wilson and he must have thought seriously about retiring from the first-class game before the 1921 season began. However, when Yorkshire approached him, as in previous seasons, to join the county side in the August school vacation, Rockley did not hesitate in accepting. It turned out to be an excellent decision. Although Yorkshire finished a disappointing third in the Championship, defeated more by the bad weather than by superior opponents, Rockley Wilson had an outstanding season. Once more appearing in only eight Championship matches, he headed Yorkshire's bowling averages with 41 wickets at a mere 11.34. He played in a further two first-class matches for Yorkshire, against the Australians at Bramall Lane in July, and against MCC in the Scarborough Festival. In all matches his haul was 51 wickets at 11.19, putting him comfortably at the head of the national bowling averages. In the match against the Australians at Bramall Lane, Wilson took three for 24 and three for 35 and had the satisfaction of trapping Warwick Armstrong, the Australian skipper (and himself a leg break bowler), lbw for low scores in both innings. Yorkshire were badly beaten however, collapsing in their second innings from 92 for two to 113 all out against the speed of Gregory and the wiles of Arthur Mailey. The more notable Wilson bowling performances in the Championship were five for 54 and nine in the match against Nottinghamshire; seven for 32 off 23 overs against Middlesex, the Champions-to-be, who were dismissed for 82, when, according to *Wisden,* he "never bowled better in his life"; four for 4 off 7.1 overs against Essex; and eleven wickets in the match against Sussex, the last of the Championship season, including seven for 67 off 37 overs in the first innings. Such an outstanding set of bowling performances in such a short period within a season can rarely have been bettered. Part-time cricketer as he may have been, they show what a contribution Rockley Wilson made to the Yorkshire side in the closing weeks of the 1921 season. *Wisden* put it this way. "Not only did he do excellent work himself, but his steadiness and impeccable length made the other bowlers more formidable than they would have been without his help."

Wilson was by now reconciled to his limitations as a batsman. He was usually ten or eleven. In 1921 he had only five innings in the Championship, scoring 81 runs at an average of 20.25. Over sixty of his runs were scored in two innings. Against Nottinghamshire at Huddersfield in the match in which Wilson took nine Nottinghamshire wickets, he scored 32 and contributed to a ninth wicket stand of 44 with Roy Kilner, when Yorkshire's first innings was teetering, that helped to put the county into a winning position. In the drawn Roses match at Headingley, he made his highest score of the season, 33 not out in a total of 489. In all matches Wilson's batting average fell to a more realistic 12.42.

The repercussions of the tour of Australia may have affected selection of the sides for the various traditional end-of-season fixtures in 1921. We know that Rockley Wilson had offended many of the cricket 'establishment', not so much by what he had said in his reports as by the upset they had inadvertently caused. He could have been more circumspect in his reporting. Time may have passed but any souring of relations within the international cricket community was to be deplored at Lord's. Rockley played for Yorkshire against the MCC in the opening fixture of the Scarborough Festival but he was not included in the Gentlemen's side to meet the Players at Scarborough, despite the outstanding season he had just enjoyed. As he had appeared in the corresponding fixture in 1919 and 1920, and as the 1921 match was to be George Hirst's last in first-class cricket and during which he celebrated his fiftieth birthday, Rockley must have been disappointed at being overlooked. Nor was he chosen for C.I.Thornton's XI to meet the Australian tourists at Scarborough or for the Rest of England team to play the champions, Middlesex, at The Oval. Were these omissions the price the authorities exacted for Wilson having blotted his copybook in Australia, or in modern parlance "brought the game into disrepute"? We cannot know. However, the fact that Percy Fender, who had been recalled to the England side for the Fourth and Fifth Tests against the Australians, was included in all three of the end of season games for which Rockley was overlooked, perhaps points against the punishment theory. The most likely explanation is his age. Whatever the explanation, his omission from the Gentlemen and

Players match was not to prove a permanent banishment for he was again selected for the Scarborough Festival fixture in 1922.

Geoffrey Wilson took over the Yorkshire captaincy from David Burton in 1922. Another Trinity College, Cambridge man, he had first appeared for Yorkshire in 1919 while still at the University and then played in a handful of games in 1921. Though he was an outstanding fielder, Geoffrey Wilson was not a good enough batsman to have held down a place in the strong Yorkshire side, but Yorkshire had need of another amateur to take over the captaincy and Geoffrey Wilson was invited to fill the bill. He could, of course, look to such sages as Wilfred Rhodes, the senior professional, and Emmott Robinson for advice as and when the need arose: stories have it that it was often the sages rather than the captain who took crucial decisions on the field of play. In the event, 1922 proved to be an excellent season for Yorkshire. They were county champions once more in what was to prove the first of four successive Championship-winning seasons, three of them with Geoffrey Wilson as captain.

Rockley Wilson was again a regular member of the team in the school vacation, again appearing in eight Championship fixtures. He also played in three other first-class matches. His was a much less successful season, however, as he took only 16 wickets in the Championship, though still at an excellent average of 17.56. He finished fifth in the Yorkshire bowling averages, behind Wilfred Rhodes, George Macaulay, Roy Kilner and Abram Waddington. In all first-class matches he took 26 wickets at 15.84. In only one match did he achieve five wickets or more in an innings, taking five for 91 off 49.3 overs against Surrey at The Oval. His batting average slumped to a mere 3.50 in the County Championship, and 6.14 in all matches.

However, the season was memorable for Wilson in one respect. When Geoffrey Wilson fell ill with appendicitis during the Roses match in August, the first of Rockley Wilson's appearances in 1922 for the county, Rockley took over the captaincy. As it turned out, Geoffrey Wilson had to miss the rest of the season and Rockley Wilson captained the side in all nine of Yorkshire's remaining fixtures. D.C.F.Burton might have been recalled in such an emergency, but Rockley was in the side, was an amateur and therefore was the obvious choice. His captaincy experience was relatively limited though, as we have seen, he had proved a capable and determined captain of Cambridge in 1902. His tactical insights were coupled with an appreciation of the strengths and weaknesses of both the opposition and his own side. There had been signs of ruthlessness in his captaincy, for example in the way he sought to overcome the weakness of the Cambridge bowling attack, which would have appealed to his Yorkshire team-mates. The captaincy of Yorkshire might have been a sinecure for some previous amateurs pitched into that position, but this was certainly not the case for Rockley Wilson, even in a team that included such seasoned professionals as Rhodes and Emmott Robinson. He would have relished the opportunity to apply his acute cricketing brain and knowledge of the game to the challenges of leading a Championship-topping team. Rockley proved to be an astute if rather cautious substitute for his namesake, earning the respect of his professional team-mates for his obvious tactical awareness (not a strong point of Geoffrey Wilson) and the way he handled the powerful Yorkshire bowling attack - though like many other bowler-captains, Rockley bowled himself notably less than his regular captain might have done, Roy Kilner being the bowler who benefited most from this modesty. Of the seven Championship matches in which Rockley Wilson was captain, three were won, one lost, two drawn and one abandoned after only 12 minutes play – this match, against Essex, clinched the Championship – and Rockley had the honour and good fortune of bringing the Championship back to Headingley.

In the Roses match at Old Trafford, when Rockley Wilson took over the captaincy from his namesake, he was involved in a most controversial last wicket partnership with Wilfred Rhodes. The bare facts are that Yorkshire needed 132 in their second innings of a low scoring match to win. When Rockley Wilson, last man because of Geoffrey Wilson's absence, joined Rhodes the score was 108 for eight: Lancashire had claimed the extra half-hour and seemed set for victory themselves. Indeed, the rest of the Yorkshire team had left the ground to begin the journey to Gloucester for the next match, never expecting other than defeat for their side. At the ground tension increased as Yorkshire's score inched upwards and, by the final over, four runs were still required for victory. Although one of the remaining deliveries was a no-ball, Rhodes made no serious attempt to get the runs required and the match finished with Yorkshire two runs short of their target. Wilfred Rhodes was 48 not out, Rockley Wilson two not out after seven overs of stonewalling. Referring afterwards to this match, Herbert Sutcliffe commented: "We knew E.R.Wilson was about the best 'flighty' bowler then playing cricket, but we always joked about his ability as a batsman until that memorable game. Afterwards, we said, with the fullest justification that in him we had a batsman who could set his teeth and stay there when there was a need for someone to stay."[86]

There was much criticism of Rhodes in the Press. He explained himself thus in a speech he gave on the occasion of another Roses match: "I expect you will say we should have gone for a win. But I say that after doing our job well for half an hour, why take the risk and undo all the good work in the last over? We had already got points for a first innings lead, and as things turned out, these were invaluable in helping Yorkshire to win the Championship in that year."[87] In a later newspaper article, Rhodes added the interesting observation that there was no discussion between himself and Wilson as to how they should go about their task: "I expected he thought I was old enough to know what to do and I certainly thought he was. I may as well say I made up my mind to play for a draw, and play for a draw we both did."[88] It is quite remarkable that the acting captain, as Wilson was in the absence of his namesake, and the senior and much respected senior professional, did not think the situation, which was clearly extremely tense, called for at least the occasional mid-pitch discussion. One must assume from this incident that, however different their backgrounds and personalities, Rockley Wilson shared some of Wilfred Rhodes' tough approach to the game, at least when the stakes were high. And he was no stranger himself to criticism, as we have seen in the account of the 1920/21 Test series in Australia.

As a footnote to this memorable game, William Ringrose, Yorkshire's scorer, later recounted how he had travelled to Gloucester in the company of Rhodes, Wilson and the journalist James Staunton. It was an all-night train journey "but it passed most pleasantly for we were generously entertained by Mr E.R.Wilson. He has a wonderful knowledge of the game and it was interesting to listen to him and Wilfred Rhodes."[89] One can imagine how today's coaches would have regarded this as preparation for a match on the following day, however interesting the conversation

---

86   Herbert Sutcliffe, *For England and Yorkshire*, Edward Arnold, 1935, p.76.
87   Sidney Rogerson, *Wilfred Rhodes*, Hollis and Carter, 1960, p.19.
88   Ibid., p.21. It should be added that Rhodes also said at this later time that he wished he had gone for the runs.
89   *Yorkshire Evening Post*, 15 August, 1936.

may have been: but long and inconvenient journeys were part of the life of first-class cricketers in the 1920s.

The three end-of-season matches in which Wilson captained Yorkshire were all drawn. In the match against MCC at Scarborough Rockley and Waddington shared a useful last wicket stand of 34 in Yorkshire's first innings total of 337 and Rockley then took three for 30 off 15 overs as MCC were dismissed for 180. But MCC hung on at 130 for seven wickets in their second innings to deny Yorkshire victory. In the Gentlemen v Players match at Scarborough, Rockley Wilson's last appearance in a representative match, he failed to score in both his innings (though was not out in one), took a couple of wickets in the Players' first innings and then that of Jack Hobbs, the only wicket to fall in the Player's second innings. At The Oval for Yorkshire against the Rest of England, Rockley also had little success with the bat but he took four for 30 in the Rest's only completed innings in which Jack Hobbs scored a masterly 100 out of 207. While his own performances in these matches were not outstanding, Rockley no doubt relished these further opportunities to lead the side that had won the Championship so convincingly.

For Yorkshire, 1923 was a wonderful season. They were champions again and overwhelming so. With a powerful batting line-up and a varied and high-quality bowling attack backed by efficient fielding, Yorkshire lost only one match of the 32 played in the Championship and only one of 35 matches in all. (They won 25 championship matches, more than any other side before or since.) The one defeat was off Nottinghamshire at Headingley in June by the slender margin of three runs. The team developed into a ruthless match-winning combination. The uncompromising way in which Yorkshire went about their business did not appeal to all their opponents however, and there were even complaints about unsporting behaviour, including picking the seam of the ball and deliberate slow scoring. There was, as one Yorkshire cricket historian later put it, "a growing conviction among some spectators and some players that success was an inherent right and failure a blasphemy against God and nature."[90] The growing hostility was to erupt in the following season when Middlesex threatened to discontinue their fixtures with Yorkshire.

---

90   Derek Hodgson, *The Official History of Yorkshire County Cricket Club*, The Crowood Press, 1989, p.114.

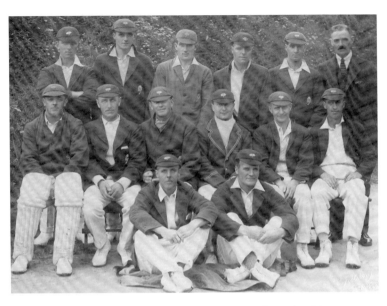

*The Yorkshire side of 1923, which took the Championship,
winning twenty-five matches.
Standing (l to r): M.Leyland, G.G.Macaulay, A.Waddington, N.Kilner, H.Sutcliffe,
W.Ringrose (scorer).
Seated: A.Dolphin, W.Rhodes, E.R.Wilson, G.Wilson (captain), E.Robinson,
P.Holmes.
On the ground: E.Oldroyd, R.Kilner.
This was Rockley Wilson's last season in first-class cricket.*

The 1923 season was a disappointing one for Rockley Wilson and was to prove his last in first-class cricket. Although he played in seven Championship games in the August school vacation, he took only ten wickets at 26.10 and dropped to sixth in the county averages. His best return was three for 46 in his first match in Lancashire's first innings at Bradford, five wickets in the whole match. His other wickets this season came in ones and twos and there were several innings in which he did not bowl at all. Rockley played one or two useful knocks at the bottom of the order. One such occasion was in the final Championship match of the season, at Taunton, against Somerset. Rockley and Arthur Dolphin put on 31 for the last wicket in Yorkshire's first innings to take their score from 149 for nine to 180, a lead of 46, from which position Yorkshire went on to win by seven wickets. Rockley finished with, for a tail ender, a presentable batting average of 14.60 in the Championship. As in 1922, Rockley Wilson deputised for his captain in three Championship matches when Geoffrey Wilson was out of the side with an injured hand.

Outside the Championship, Rockley had a quiet game for Yorkshire in the drawn match against MCC at the Scarborough Cricket Festival scoring no runs and taking no wickets. The final match of the season on 14, 15 and 17 September was Yorkshire's game against the Rest of England at The Oval. It was to be Rockley Wilson's final appearance in first-class cricket. As so often with these end-of-season fixtures at this time however, the match was drawn. Indeed it was disappointing as a contest, effectively a one innings match. Yorkshire scored 430 for four wickets in their first innings, Percy Holmes top scoring with 99 and Rockley of course not being called upon to bat. The strong Rest eleven were then dismissed for 273 in their only innings, Rockley taking two for 30.

Taking the season as a whole, Wilson had a batting average of 12.16 and took just 12 wickets at 27.41. Summing up, while his batting might occasionally still have been of value, Rockley Wilson's bowling had clearly fallen away. And it was his bowling that had been his greatest asset over the years.

Rockley was now 44 years old and his age was beginning to become more apparent, even among the relatively elderly sides which were characteristic of county cricket in the twenties. Of course, Wilfred Rhodes was older and still going strong – he topped the Yorkshire bowling averages in 1923 with 127 wickets at 11.49 – but as a professional he had more incentive to do so than Rockley. Yorkshire were now able to call on a strong and varied attack throughout the season. Roy Kilner, Abram Waddington, Emmott Robinson and George Macaulay had all established themselves in the side since the end of the First World War. We do not know whether Yorkshire indicated to Rockley at the end of the 1923 season that he should not expect to be called upon in 1924, or whether he decided himself to call it a day as a first-class cricketer and concentrate on his teaching career. Whatever the facts, it had probably become clear to him that his first-class career was over. In that career, spanning intermittently twenty-four seasons, Rockley Wilson took 467 wickets in first-class cricket at an average of 17.63. For Yorkshire, his tally was 197 wickets at an average of 15.76. These are excellent figures by any standard.

Chapter Eleven
Later Years

Although he had retired, Rockley Wilson found himself making an important contribution to the county club in the following 1924 season when again Yorkshire won the Championship. Yorkshire's success was bought at the price of a further deterioration in the club's relationship with certain other counties, particularly Middlesex and Surrey. The flashpoint was the match at Bramall Lane against Middlesex when aggressive appealing and apparent dissent at the umpires' decisions, by Waddington in particular, provoked the crowd into barracking the Middlesex players and to other unruly behaviour. *Wisden* reported: "For some reason, the Sheffield crowd, forgetting their old reputation for good sportsmanship, barracked more or less persistently all through the game, making the atmosphere almost unbearable." The reasons were fairly obvious. A Middlesex side containing several amateurs with public school and Oxbridge backgrounds, based at Lord's, the headquarters of the cricket 'establishment', was never going to be a favourite of the Bramall Lane crowd – or of many of the Yorkshire players for that matter – especially after the innings defeat that Middlesex had inflicted on Yorkshire in the earlier fixture at Lord's. Criticism from that quarter of the way Yorkshire played the game was bound to annoy many of the county's supporters. Anyhow, the outcome of the rumpus was that the umpires, H.R.Butt and W.Reeves, reported the incidents to Lord's and Middlesex backed up their protests by threatening to discontinue the fixture with Yorkshire for the 1925 season.

An MCC committee was set up to enquire into the matter and concluded that the umpires' complaints were justified. Waddington was persuaded to write a letter of apology to MCC and Rockley Wilson was asked by Yorkshire to use his good offices to help find a way to re-establish good relations between the two counties. He must have smiled wryly at the irony of a request to help deal with the results of unseemly barracking by his own county's crowd, when he had been subjected to much more merciless and personal barracking in Australia just three years before. However, Rockley was well equipped for the task. He was respected at Lord's and was acquainted with a number of the Middlesex amateurs and more aware than them of the sensitivities (or prejudices) of working class northerners, whether professional players or spectators. With a foot in both camps, as it were, and his personal qualities Rockley Wilson was able to bring about a restoration of relations, though not without the ploy of threatening that if Middlesex were to drop Yorkshire for one year, Yorkshire would drop Middlesex for fifty.[91] Whether or not this clinched the matter, the Middlesex threat not to play Yorkshire in 1925 was withdrawn.

One consequence of the disturbances and disharmony that marred Yorkshire's third successive Championship in 1924 was Geoffrey Wilson's resignation as captain. He did not favour a "win at all costs" approach to the game and his own shortcomings as a player in a team of such obvious champions must have added to his discomfiture. Rockley Wilson liked the man and he would have had mixed feelings about his departure after three successive Championship wins.

Rockley kept loosely in touch with Yorkshire cricket thereafter and made occasional journeys to Leeds to watch matches, visit his nephews and friends, and occasionally to speak at cricket functions. Bob Appleyard recalled being visited by Rockley in 1952 when Bob was seriously ill in Leeds Infirmary with advanced tuberculosis.[92] Rockley had a genuine concern for any cricketer who had suffered some personal misfortune. On a more social level, in October 1956, in what was to be the last year of his life, he travelled to Leeds for a reunion of the four Championship-winning sides of 1922-1925, organised by the Northern Cricket Society. He was not an official speaker but was asked by the Yorkshire President, Sir William Worsley, to say a few words. We can be sure Rockley would have kept his companions amused with his recollections and stories. In a letter to his nephew David Wilson, Rockley said that Sir William commented, "All agreed that yours was the speech of the evening." Like any public speaker, Rockley liked to hear appreciation of his efforts.

Rockley Wilson's own career in first-class cricket may have been over after the 1923 season but he continued to play club cricket, as

---

91   As reported in E.W.Swanton, *Follow On*, Collins, 1977, p.192.
92   In conversation with the writer.

J.T.McGaw's ground at St Leonard's Forest, Horsham was a home of high-class club cricket in the twenties and thirties. Rockley Wilson is here second from the left in the front row, his nephew R.M. on the back row at the right, and "Old Man" McGaw in the centre of the front row.

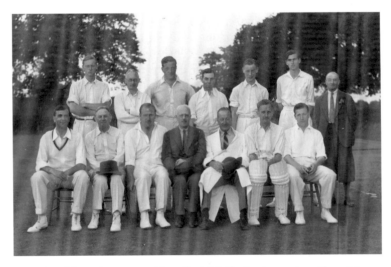

Rockley Wilson, here second from the left in the front row, played in matches involving the Dewhurst family at the Vale of Clwyd ground at Denbigh in the twenties.

he had before and during his career with Yorkshire, on a fairly regular basis and for a variety of sides. He was in his element, enjoying the opportunity to continue playing cricket and the company and hospitality of his many friends, cosseted, it has to be said, against the economic problems that Britain was experiencing as the 1920s wore on. Accounts and stories of his appearances in club cricket in this later period of his cricketing life demonstrate that Rockley retained all his bowling skills, even beyond his fiftieth year. To give a few examples, from 1925 until 1931 he played regularly for the McGaw family team on a picturesque country house ground at St Leonard's Forest, Horsham. "Old Man" John Thoburn McGaw, shown in the photograph on the previous page, who owned extensive properties in Australia and Argentina, was a keen all-round sportsman and an excellent wicket-keeper. (Rockley referred to him as "flypaper McGaw".) Trained as an engineer, he used his mechanical skills to design scoreboards for grounds with which he was associated, including Charterhouse School and Christ's Hospital. He was able to attract teams of the calibre of Free Foresters, Charterhouse Friars, Old Malvernians, the Cryptics and the Royal Navy to play his own invitation elevens. Over the seven seasons Rockley played for these elevens, he achieved the astonishing figures of 201 wickets from 1,231.3 overs at an average of 9.7 and with five wickets or more in an innings on scores of occasions, ten or more in no fewer than eleven matches. He also took a large number of catches, mainly at first slip. Not only is this an impressive record of his performances on the field of play, it shows how committed Rockley could be to clubs and friends who played the game as he liked it to be played and in agreeable surroundings. Another favourite venue was the Vale of Clwyd Cricket Club ground at Denbigh. At the invitation of his friend Gerard Powys Dewhurst, Rockley played for the local side in the Clwyd Cricket Week on a number of occasions in the 1920s against such teams as Shropshire Gentlemen, Royal Welch Fusiliers, and Old Cheltonians. Rockley would stay at Gerard Dewhurst's country house at nearby Llandegla for the duration of the Cricket Week.[93] Playing against Old Cheltonians in 1927, he

---

93   Rockley Wilson had first played with Gerard Dewhurst, and with two of his brothers, for Northern Nomads sides in the early 1900s. Of the brothers Harry Dewhurst was the best-known cricketer; he played for Cheshire as well as for club sides. Gerard was better known at soccer: he played for England against Wales in 1895. The family had made its fortune in the cotton industry (Sylko sewing thread was one of the business' best known products) though Gerard Dewhurst's business interests went beyond those of the family cotton firm. In later life he was chairman of Williams Deacon's Bank.

was asked to keep the runs down and began with 14 consecutive maidens. After 27 overs only two singles had been taken off him, one from a misfield, and he ended with the extraordinary figures of seven for 12 off 36 overs of which 28 were maidens. And this was a man of 48 years. For the Butterflies at Charterhouse on a scorching day in 1928, he bowled unchanged for 28 overs of which 14 were maidens and took seven for 29.

Although fame always sat lightly on Rockley's shoulders, he could be annoyed if his reputation appeared to be besmirched. During I Zingari's innings in a match against Aldershot Command, Rockley took exception to some disparaging remarks about his batting by an opponent, a Minor Counties player, who did not recognise his pedigree. When this man's time came to bat, Rockley teased him for half an hour with a succession of perfectly flighted, good length balls pitched just outside the off stump which the batsman frequently played at without getting an edge. When a team-mate commiserated on the bowler's bad luck, Rockley retorted "Bad luck, bad luck. Keep the little bastard there another half hour. Make him look a fool. Make him look a fool." Rockley Wilson could never tolerate what he considered boorish or unseemly behaviour on the field of play. One trembles to think what his reaction would be to the sledging, excessive appealing and over-the-top celebrations of the fall of a wicket that are such features of modern day cricket. He only appealed himself if he was confident that a batsman was out. It is recounted that he immediately followed up one appeal with "Not out, very sorry, nowhere near, nowhere near." The wicketkeeper judged that the ball could not have pitched more than half an inch off the wicket. Occasionally in the later years of his cricketing life, Rockley produced a memorable performance with the bat. In 1935, for instance, he scored a century in a match at Fosseway, another favourite venue of his, for Myles Kenyon's XI, and 50 for the Green Jackets against Eton at Lord's. [94]

In 1933 Rockley Wilson made his final appearance for MCC, against the Gentlemen of Ireland in a two-day match at Lord's, at the age of 54 years. He took six for 49 off 23.2 overs in Ireland's first innings, another remarkable feat of bowling and stamina. But it was off the field that his presence was mainly felt at cricket's headquarters. Rockley was regularly consulted by MCC for advice.

---

94   This material on club appearances is from R.L.Arrowsmith, E.R.Wilson: Part II, *Cricket Quarterly*, Vol. 6, 1968, pp.6-7, supplemented by David Wilson's papers.

He served after the Second World War on the MCC Arts and Library sub-committee, as natural a role for him within the MCC set-up as can be imagined. Of greater significance, however, for the game at large was his work in 1944 with Harry Altham, his colleague from Winchester days, assisting R.S.Rait Kerr, the MCC Secretary, with the drafting of a new Code of the Laws of Cricket. The Code ultimately adopted in 1947 owes much to Rockley's scholarly input to the drafting process.[95] In a more social context, Rockley was a frequent visitor to Lord's, whether to watch matches or merely to use the members' facilities, where he enjoyed the company of his wide circle of cricket friends and acquaintances.

He continued with his teaching career at Winchester College, of course, and, until 1929, with his responsibilities for cricket and cricket coaching which he finally surrendered to Harry Altham, then ten years his junior, though he continued to bowl in the nets at Winchester until 1946 when he was 67 years old. He was a house tutor in Furley House and had ambitions to be housemaster but was considered unsuitable for such a position. He certainly had no obvious administrative skills and organisation, even of his own affairs, was not a strong point. In November, 1945 the time finally arrived for him to give up the teaching duties which he had willingly continued during the war years.

After retirement, Rockley was a regular spectator at Winchester's matches and took a close interest in the team's performances, as ever quick to impart encouragement and advice and to engage in conversation and reminiscences. He contributed in other ways than cricket to the life of Winchester College. He was an active member of the Wykehamist Society, contributing occasionally to the Society's journal, and on the occasion of his sixtieth birthday, exchanging celebratory poems in Latin with Bob Arrowsmith in its pages. In 1956 he completed, with H.A.Jackson, a life-long friend, the laborious task of updating the 1901-1946 edition of the Register of boys who attended the school. He apparently had a yen for this kind of work, for in 1945 he had completed, for the Free Foresters Cricket Club, an up-to-date Members List and Club Records.

During his early years as a teacher, Rockley lived in the school. After returning from the First World War, he bought a house at 16

---

95   Referring to the contribution of Altham and Wilson, Rait Kerr said that both have "given up more time than they could possibly afford to help me over difficulties": R.S.Rait Kerr, *The Laws of Cricket*, Longmans Green, 1950, p.xvi.

St James Lane which he crammed with his collections of cricket books and other cricketana, silver and furniture. There is a splendid story of George Hirst dining with Rockley after he had retired as cricket coach at Eton and on the occasion of the annual Winchester v Eton match. Having admired a painting of Fuller Pilch, Hirst is said to have pointed to the gap between Pilch's bat and pads and remarked: "Ah think ah could put wun through there." Doubtless Rockley would have concurred.

Rockley shared his home for a number of years with his sister Phyllis, who also had a love of beautiful and old things. Some time after the Second World War failing health meant that Phyllis had to be looked after in a mental home in Perth. Rockley visited her from time to time despite the distance and the trying circumstances. Now living alone, he was helped by a housekeeper and by "my man Rayment" whose services were mainly as handyman and chauffeur.[96]

The end of an innings

Inevitably Rockley Wilson became something of an institution not just at Winchester College but also around the town. In his final years he continued to interest himself in cricket at Winchester and further afield, and, largely through correspondence, to keep in touch with his extended family. He had had some heart trouble, but when the end came on 21 July, 1957 it was a shock. Only on 1 July he had written a long letter to his nephew David Wilson in which he described in some detail the performances of Winchester College in four inter-school matches, a lunch he had recently provided for ten guests, and his plan to attend a wedding in London later in the month. He had signed himself off "Well, but a poor walker." A few days later he had been guest of honour at a dinner of the Old Wykehamists when he had been presented with a silver salver as a mark of the Society's appreciation of his great services to the school. Shortly before his death Rockley had travelled to Scotland, presumably to visit his sister Phyllis, and had also made plans to go to Leeds for the Test match against the West Indies scheduled to start on 25 July.

---

96   Patrick Maclure in *The Best of Rockley,* privately published 1998, p.4, refers to Rockley Wilson's "man" as Raymond but before his death David Wilson, Rockley's nephew, assured the writer that his name was Rayment. David Wilson, a frequent visitor to Rockley's home, added "I liked him [Rayment] very much."

Rockley Wilson died of heart failure at his home in Winchester, aged 78 years. The many obituaries reviewed the career of this remarkable cricketer, none more comprehensively, as might be expected, than the obituary in the 1958 *Wisden*, which described him as "one of the best amateur slow right-arm bowlers of his time" adding that "immaculate length and cleverly-disguised variations of pace made Wilson difficult to punish." Others added more human touches to their account. Thus from the obituary in *The Times* on 22 July, 1957 already referred to: "He was a personality both on and off the field in a day when the word had not been debased and to achieve real fame required real skill and force of character. Both of these Wilson had." And from Sir Pelham Warner's obituary in *The Cricketer*, 3 August: "Wilson possessed a delightful personality and to talk cricket with him was an education. Modest to a degree, he never attempted to lay down the law and his sense of humour was great." The obituary by Harry Altham, his friend and colleague at Winchester College, in the *Hampshire Chronicle* of 27 July, reprinted in *The Wykehamist* of 15 October, included this: "But Rockley Wilson was much more than a fine cricketer: he was a great personality in his own right. Few men can have been more often quoted among his friends, whether for story or repartee. The latter could be devastating, for he did not always suffer fools gladly, but increasingly with the years the abiding impression which he left will be of friendliness, of humour and of a kind heart." Later his friend Bob Arrowsmith remembered him this way: "He was a man with natural gifts which might have won him distinction in many fields and which did win him distinction as a cricketer. But more than that he is remembered with deep gratitude and affection by many generations of Wykehamists and by many others, both in the cricket world and outside, as a kind, generous warm-hearted man, a loyal friend and an endlessly entertaining and stimulating companion."[97]

Rockley's funeral on 25 July in the College Chapel was attended by a large congregation of friends and representatives of the school, the town, and the world of cricket. The family mourners were two of Rockley's nephews, Ralph Macro Wilson and Commodore Edward Raynold, R.N. (retd). Rockley was buried in the Magdalen Hill Cemetery, just outside Winchester. Later, Rockley's life was commemorated with memorial services, first on 1 August, 1957 most appropriately at St John's Wood Church, the cricketers'

---

97   R.L.Arrowsmith, E.R.Wilson Part II, op.cit., p.76.

church close to Lord's, and then on 14 August at St Mary's Church, Bolsterstone, the village of his birth.

The plain headstone to Rockley's grave bears the simple inscription "Evelyn Rockley Wilson, 25 March 1879 - 21 July 1957." There is nothing to tell the visitor that the headstone marks the final resting place of a devoted Wykehamist and a gifted cricketer. Some years before, however, a tent (as pavilions are known at Winchester) had been built on the College playing field known as Gater Field in his honour. A commemorative plaque, unveiled by Rockley's friend Sir Hubert Ashton on the opening of the pavilion on 28 May 1966, reads:

This tent has been built in memory of Rockley Wilson (1879 to 1957)

who devoted 54 years of his life to Winchester and is remembered by

cricketers with affection and gratitude.

It is a worthy tribute to a remarkable cricketer and a singular man.

Acknowledgements

The writer is most grateful to Jocelyn Wilson, wife of the late David Wilson, who was the son of Clement Eustace Macro Wilson and Rockley Wilson's nephew; and to Christopher Wilson, David Wilson's son, for the loan of various of David Wilson's papers, photographs and Press cuttings relating to Clement and Rockley Wilson. When drawn on by the writer, these are referred to as the Wilson papers. The writer wishes warmly to thank David Jeater of the Association of Cricket Statisticians and Historians for his encouragement and careful editing of the text; Zahra Ridge for her work on the cover design; Philip Bailey for his statistical assistance; Roger Mann and the Wilson family for help with illustrations; Peter Hartland and Ian Grey for their proof-reading. Other persons the writer wishes to thank are Glenys Williams, MCC Archivist and Historian; Susanne Foster, Deputy Archivist, Winchester College; Rusty Mclean, Archivist, Rugby School; Peter Griffiths, Roger Heavens, Andrew Hignell, Bobi Owen and Christopher Finch.

Bibliography

This bibliography lists the main sources consulted on the life and career of Rockley Wilson. Specific sources are footnoted throughout the text. Quotations in the text for which no source is given are from documents among the Wilson papers.

Family history
Phyllis Crossland, The Wilsons of Broomhead Hall, *Yorkshire History*, Vol.1, 1995.
David Wilson, *The History of the Wilson Family*, 1991, mimeo, Sheffield City Library.
David Wilson, *A Century of the Sheffield Collegiate Cricket Club*, privately published 1981.

Previous publications on Rockley Wilson
R.L.Arrowsmith, E.R.Wilson: Part I and Part II, *The Cricket Quarterly*, Vol.6, 1967/68.
Jeremy Malies, *Great Characters from Cricket's Golden Age*, Robson Books, 2000.
Patrick Maclure, *The Best of Rockley*, privately published, 1998. (An extensive selection of anecdotes about Rockley Wilson.)
All of these authors benefited from information provided by David Wilson, Rockley's nephew.

Other noteworthy reminiscences of Rockley Wilson
R.C.Robertson-Glasgow, *More Cricket Prints*, T.Werner Laurie, 1948.
Irving Rosenwater, Rockley Wilson, *The White Rose*, May 1998.
Irving Rosenwater, *Cricket Books: Great Collectors of the Past*, privately published, 1976.
E.W.Swanton, The Wit and Wisdom of Rockley Wilson, *The Cricketer*, July 1979.
E.W.Swanton, Characters of Yesterday: Rockley Wilson, *The Cricketer*, February 1997.

Yorkshire cricket

Lord Hawke, *Recollections and Reminiscences*, Williams and Norgate, 1924.

Peter Thomas, *Yorkshire Cricketers: 1839-1939*, Derek Hodgson Publisher, 1973.

Reverend R.S.Holmes, *The History of Yorkshire County Cricket, 1833-1903*, Archibald Constable, 1904.

C.M.Marston, *A Century of Cricket at Bramall Lane, 1855-1955*, Greenup and Thompson (for Sheffield United Cricket Club), 1955.

A.W.Pullin ("Old Ebor"), *History of Yorkshire County Cricket, 1903-1923*, Chorley and Pickersgill, 1924.

Derek Hodgson, *The Official History of Yorkshire County Cricket Club*, The Crowood Press, 1989.

Anthony Woodhouse, *The History of Yorkshire County Cricket Club*, Christopher Helm, 1989.

Anthony Woodhouse, *A Who's Who of Yorkshire County Cricket Club*, Breedon Books, 1992.

Other useful sources

Ronald Bowen, *Cricket: A History of its Growth and Development Throughout the World*, Eyre and Spottiswoode, 1970.

Neville Cardus, *The Roses Matches, 1919-1939*, Souvenir Press, 1982.

George Chesterton and Hubert Doggart, *Oxford and Cambridge Cricket*, Willow Books, 1989.

Christopher Douglas, *Douglas Jardine: Spartan Cricketer*, Methuen (paperback), 2003.

P.G.H.Fender, *Defending the Ashes,* Chapman and Hall, 1921.

W.F.Ford, *A History of the Cambridge University Cricket Club,* Wm. Blackwood, 1902.

E.H.Hendren, *Big Cricket,* Hodder and Stoughton, 1934.

Jack Hobbs, *My Life Story*, The Star Publications, 1935.

J.M.Kilburn, *The Scarborough Cricket Festival,* Scarborough Cricket Club, 1948.

Sir Henry Leveson Gower, *Off and On the Field,* Stanley Paul, 1953.

E.B.Noel, *Winchester College Cricket*, Williams and Norgate, 1926.

C.H.Parkin, *Cricket Triumphs and Troubles*, C.Nicholls, 1936.

Sidney Rogerson, *Wilfred Rhodes*, Hollis and Carter, 1960.

Richard Streeton, *P.G.H.Fender: a Biography*, Faber and Faber, 1981.

Herbert Sutcliffe, *For England and Yorkshire*, Edward Arnold, 1935.

P.F.Warner (ed.), *Cricket: The Badminton Library*, Longmans Green, 1920.

P.F.Warner, *Long Innings*, George G. Harrap and Co., 1951.

The writer has used material from *Wisden Cricketers' Almanacks, Yorkshire County Cricket Club Yearbooks, The Cricketer*, and national and local newspapers, both English and Australian.

Appendix One
Some Statistics

Test cricket

Rockley Wilson played in one Test match, for England v Australia at Sydney in the 1920/21 season. He scored ten runs in two innings and took three wickets for 36 off 20.3 overs, five of which were maidens. He took no catches. The full score of this match is given in Appendix Two.

First-class cricket: Batting and Fielding

		M	I	NO	R	HS	Ave	100	50	Ct
1899	Eng	13	23	1	649	117*	29.50	1	3	13
1900	Eng	15	25	2	632	82	27.47	-	5	13
1901	Eng	8	15	0	469	118	31.26	1	1	12
1901	USA	2	4	0	27	9	6.75	-	-	2
1901/02	WI	12	17	1	402	81	25.12	-	2	12
1902	Eng	14	25	3	438	142	19.90	1	1	17
1911/12	Arg	3	6	1	129	67*	25.80	-	1	4
1913	Eng	7	9	3	192	104*	32.00	1	-	2
1914	Eng	2	3	1	14	13*	7.00	-	-	3
1919	Eng	11	12	2	165	51	16.50	-	1	5
1920	Eng	12	14	5	121	39*	13.44	-	-	9
1920/21	Aus	7	8	0	124	56	15.50	-	1	2
1921	Eng	10	8	1	87	33*	12.42	-	-	7
1922	Eng	11	14	7	43	13*	6.14	-	-	2
1923	Eng	9	7	1	73	24	12.16	-	-	3
Career		**136**	**190**	**28**	**3565**	**142**	**22.00**	**4**	**15**	**106**

Note: Wilson was dismissed 75 times caught (46%); 52 times bowled (32%); 19 times lbw; 10 times stumped and six times run out. Wilfred Rhodes took his wicket seven times, more often than any other bowler, mainly in matches at Fenner's and in Scarborough Festival games.

First-class cricket: Bowling

		O	M	R	W	BB	Ave	5i	10m
1899	Eng	377.3	105	988	36	4-49	27.44	-	-
1900	Eng	233.5	56	589	25	7-79	23.56	1	1
1901	Eng	358.2	91	917	37	7-37	24.78	3	1
1901	USA	52.2	12	152	8	5-100	19.00	1	-
1901/02	WI	414.1	144	767	67	7-16	11.44	5	1
1902	Eng	512.4	172	1061	58	5-46	18.29	3	-
1911/12	Arg	82	22	183	17	6-36	10.76	1	-
1913	Eng	176.5	64	354	18	6-89	19.66	1	-
1914	Eng	13	4	36	0	-	-	-	-
1919	Eng	321.5	108	699	40	7-46	17.47	2	-

1920	Eng	531	210	886	64	6-29	13.84	5	1
1920/21	Aus	134.3	39	290	8	2-18	36.25	-	-
1921	Eng	370	170	571	51	7-32	11.19	3	1
1922	Eng	259	106	412	26	5-91	15.84	1	-
1923	Eng	200	90	329	12	3-46	27.41	-	-
Career **5-b**		**377.3**	**105}**	**8234**	**467**	**7-16**	**17.63**	**26**	**5**
6-b		**3659.3**	**1288}**						

Notes: Overs in 1899 were five balls: in all other seasons six. Wilson took his wickets at the rate of one per 51.05 balls and conceded runs at the rate of 2.07 runs per six-ball over. Of his 467 wickets, 288 (62%) were caught; 103 (22%) were bowled; 51 lbw and 25 stumped. He secured a higher proportion of his wickets through catches than many comparable contemporaries. He took the wicket of F.T.Mann eleven times, more than any other batsman who faced him.

First-class cricket: Fifties (19)

Score	For	Opponent	Venue	Season
117*	A.J.Webbe's XI[1]	v Cambridge Univ	Fenner's	1899
70	A.J.Webbe's XI[2]	v Cambridge Univ	Fenner's	1899
55	Yorkshire[1]	v Somerset	Hull	1899
79	Yorkshire[1]	v Warwickshire	Edgbaston	1899
65	Cambridge Univ[1]	v London County	Fenner's	1900
80	Cambridge Univ[1]	v Surrey	Fenner's	1900
59	Cambridge Univ[2]	v Sussex	Fenner's	1900
60	Cambridge Univ[1]	v London County	Crystal Palace	1900
82	Cambridge Univ[2]	v Sussex	Hove	1900
57	Cambridge Univ[1]	v MCC	Lord's	1901
118	Cambridge Univ[1]	v Oxford Univ	Lord's	1901
81	R.A.Bennett's XI[1]	v Jamaica	Kingston	1901/02
71	R.A.Bennett's XI[1]	v Combined Jamaica and United Services XI	Kingston	1901/02
142	Cambridge Univ[2]	v MCC	Lord's	1902
63	Yorkshire[1]	v Worcestershire	Worcester	1902
67*	MCC[1]	v Argentina	Hurlingham	1911/12
104*	Yorkshire[1]	v Essex	Bradford	1913
51	Yorkshire[1]	v Leicestershire	Leicester	1919
56	MCC[1]	v Australian XI	Brisbane	1920/21

First-class cricket: Five Wickets in an Innings (26)

Bowling	For	Opponent	Venue	Season
33.3-6-79-7	Cambridge U	v MCC[2]	Lord's	1900
22-6-37-7	Cambridge U	v Worcestershire[1]	Fenner's	1901
34.2-13-38-7	Cambridge U	v Worcestershire[2]	Fenner's	1901
45-20-71-5	Cambridge U	v Oxford U[1]	Lord's	1901
17.3-5-100-5	B.J.T.Bosanquet's XI	v Gentlemen of Philadelphia[1]	Manheim	1901
30.3-10-39-6	R.A.Bennett's XI	v Combined Jamaica and United Services XI[1]	Kingston	1901/02
31-16-64-5	R.A.Bennett's XI	v Trinidad[1]	Port of Spain	1901/02
26.2-9-30-6	R.A.Bennett's XI	v British Guiana[1]	Georgetown	1901/02
23-7-46-7	R.A.Bennett's XI	v West Indies[1]	Georgetown	1901/02
13.2-8-16-7	R.A.Bennett's XI	v West Indies[2]	Georgetown	1901/02
43-12-114-5	Cambridge U	v H.D.G.Leveson Gower's XI[2]	Fenner's	1902
39.3-20-46-5	Cambridge U	v Surrey[1]	The Oval	1902

35-13-53-5	Cambridge U	v Oxford U[1]	Lord's	1902
21-7-36-6	MCC	v Argentina[2]	Buenos Aires	1911/12
35.2-10-89-6	Yorkshire	v Warwickshire[1]	Edgbaston	1913
18.3-9-28-6	Yorkshire	v Middlesex[2]	Lord's	1919
26.3-9-46-7	Yorkshire	v MCC[1]	Scarborough	1919
36-13-49-5	Yorkshire	v Sussex[1]	Headingley	1920
44-22-62-6	Yorkshire	v Middlesex[2]	Bradford	1920
19.4-11-29-5	Yorkshire	v Surrey[2]	The Oval	1920
25.1-18-20-5	Yorkshire	v Hampshire[1]	Portsmouth	1920
15.4-7-29-6	Yorkshire	v MCC[2]	Scarborough	1920
22-9-54-5	Yorkshire	v Nottinghamshire[1]	Huddersfield	1921
23-11-32-7	Yorkshire	v Middlesex[1]	Sheffield	1921
37-14-67-7	Yorkshire	v Sussex[1]	Hove	1921
49.3-22-91-5	Yorkshire	v Surrey[1]	The Oval	1922

Note: The index figures [1] and [2] in the two tables immediately above indicate the innings in which the feat was achieved.

Sources for all four tables: Wisden Cricketers' Almanacks, cricketarchive.com

Appendix Two
Rockley Wilson's Only Test Match

AUSTRALIA v ENGLAND
Played at Sydney Cricket Ground, February 25, 26, 28, March 1, 1921.
Australia won by nine wickets.

ENGLAND

1	J.B.Hobbs	lbw b Gregory	40	(5) c Taylor b Mailey	34
2	W.Rhodes	c Carter b Kelleway	26	run out	25
3	J.W.H.Makepeace	c Gregory b Mailey	3	c Gregory b Kelleway	7
4	E.H.Hendren	c Carter b Gregory	5	(6) st Carter b Mailey	13
5	F.E.Woolley	b McDonald	53	(1) c and b Kelleway	1
6	C.A.G.Russell	c Gregory b Mailey	19	(8) c Gregory b Armstrong	35
7	*J.W.H.T.Douglas	not out	32	c and b Mailey	68
8	P.G.H.Fender	c Gregory b Kelleway	2	(9) c Kelleway b McDonald	40
9	E.R.Wilson	c Carter b Kelleway	5	(4) st Carter b Mailey	5
10	C.H.Parkin	c Taylor b Kelleway	9	c Gregory b Mailey	36
11	†H.Strudwick	b Gregory	2	not out	5
	Extras	b 3, lb 2, w 1, nb 2	8	b 3, lb 5, nb 3	11
	Total		204		280

FoW (1): 1-54 (2), 2-70 (1), 3-74 (3), 4-76 (4), 5-125 (6), 6-161 (5), 7-164 (8), 8-172 (9), 9-201 (10), 10-204 (11)
FoW (2): 1-1 (1), 2-14 (3), 3-29 (4), 4-75 (5), 5-82 (2), 6-91 (6), 7-160 (8), 8-224 (9), 9-251 (7), 10-280 (10)

AUSTRALIA

1	H.L.Collins	c Fender b Parkin	5	c Strudwick b Wilson	37
2	W.Bardsley	c Fender b Douglas	7	not out	50
3	C.G.Macartney	c Hobbs b Fender	170	not out	2
4	J.M.Taylor	c Hendren b Douglas	32		
5	J.M.Gregory	c Strudwick b Fender	93		
6	*W.W.Armstrong	c Woolley b Fender	0		
7	J.Ryder	b Fender	2		
8	C.Kelleway	c Strudwick b Wilson	32		
9	†H.Carter	c Woolley b Fender	17		
10	A.A.Mailey	b Wilson	5		
11	E.A.McDonald	not out	3		
	Extras	b 18, lb 6, nb 2	26	b 3, nb 1	4
	Total		392	(1 wicket)	93

FoW (1): 1-16 (1), 2-22 (2), 3-89 (4), 4-287 (5), 5-287 (6), 6-313 (7), 7-356 (3), 8-384 (8), 9-384 (9), 10-392 (10)

FoW (2): 1-91 (1)

Australia Bowling

	O	M	R	W		O	M	R	W
Gregory	16.1	4	42	3	(4)	16	3	37	0
McDonald	11	2	38	1	(1)	25	3	58	1
Kelleway	20	6	27	4	(2)	14	3	29	2
Mailey	23	1	89	2	(3)	36.2	5	119	5
Ryder					(5)	2	2	0	0
Armstrong					(6)	8	2	26	1

England Bowling

	O	M	R	W		O	M	R	W
Douglas	16	0	84	2					
Parkin	19	1	83	1	(1)	9	1	32	0
Woolley	15	1	58	0	(2)	11	3	27	0
Wilson	14.3	4	28	2	(5)	6	1	8	1
Fender	20	1	90	5	(3)	1	0	2	0
Rhodes	7	0	23	0	(4)	7.2	1	20	0

Umpires: R.M.Crockett and D.A.Elder.   Toss: England

Close of Play: 1st day: Australia (1) 70-2 (Macartney 31*, Taylor 22*); 2nd day: England (2) 24-2 (Rhodes 10*, Wilson 4*); 3rd day: Australia (2) 25-0 (Collins 7*, Bardsley 17*).

Source: cricketarchive.com